PRAISE FOR *HOLY GROUND*

Castaldo speaks from his own spiritual pilgrimage about the unity between believing Catholics and faithful Evangelicals, the important differences that remain between us, and what all of this means to our witness in the world today. Great stuff!

—Timothy George, Senior Editor, *Christianity Today*

Castaldo offers a challenge for Evangelicals to recognize that their Catholic friends and family can, yes, know Jesus. He also offers insight into why so many former Catholics have found a home in the Evangelical world.

—Peter Feuerherd, author, *Holyland USA: A Catholic Ride through America's Evangelical Landscape*

Castaldo explores the dilemmas and experiences former Catholics face as they seek to move forward as Evangelicals. Well researched, up to date, and insightful, this book will enrich the most strained Catholic-Evangelical relationships.

—Dorington G. Little, Senior Pastor, First Congregational Church, Hamilton, MA

Principled and gracious, theological and practical, full of careful reasoning and warm illustrations—this is a book I will recommend to others. It does a great service to the Evangelical church. And it just might help a few Catholics too.

—Kevin DeYoung, Senior Pastor, University Reformed Church, East Lansing, MI

Castaldo knows both Catholics and Evangelicals well, has a sense of humor, writes clearly, and displays a deep knowledge of the events and doctrinal differences surrounding the Reformation. May this balanced treatment provide needed understanding for Catholics and Protestants alike.

—Ralph E. MacKenzie, coauthor, *Roman Catholics and Evangelicals: Agreements and Differences*

This is a sensitive, well-written, and helpful treatment of how to discuss one's Evangelical faith with Catholics. It lacks the edge found in many overzealous converts, yet states clearly why Castaldo chose Evangelicalism over the Catholic faith in which he was reared.

—Norman Geisler, author, *Is Rome the True Church?*

A timely, careful book which blends the pastoral, personal, and theological issues and approaches which are vital in responding to folks within and outside the Catholic community.

—David Cook, Holmes Professor, Wheaton College

Catholics are becoming Evangelicals faster than the reverse by a ratio of about three to one. What do these converts find? How should they relate to their Catholic families and friends? This is the best book I have read that chronicles such pilgrimages. And it is full of godly common sense.

—D. A. Carson, Research Professor of New Testament, Trinity Evangelical Divinity School

If you've had enough of Evangelical writers who make a straw man of the Catholic Church and then knock it down, this book is for you. Anyone trying to bridge the worlds of Evangelicalism and Catholicism will benefit from its wisdom.

—Bryan M. Litfin, author, *Getting to Know the Church Fathers: An Evangelical Introduction*

I have been looking for a book for my students to read so they can understand two issues: what it is like for Catholics to become Evangelical followers of Jesus Christ, and how these former Catholics can live and share the good news with their Catholic relatives and friends. *Holy Ground* is that book!

—Gregg R. Allison, Professor of Christian Theology, The Southern Baptist Theological Seminary

I highly recommend *Holy Ground* as a must-read for every Christian. Castaldo has done an excellent job providing insight and balance in an area that is rarely addressed. *Holy Ground* has power to change your life.

—Randal Ross, Senior Pastor, Calvary Church, Naperville, IL

How very important it is that conservative Evangelical and Catholic laypeople should relate to each other with respectful insight, on a basis of mutual understanding. And how very helpful this book is as a means to this end.

—J. I. Packer, Professor of Theology, Regent College

Even those with no Catholic background will appreciate Castaldo's wit and wisdom as he tiptoes through the land mines in *Holy Ground.*

—Collin Hansen, author, *Young, Restless, Reformed: A Journalist's Journey with the New Calvinists*

Castaldo clearly and charitably explains to Evangelicals the diverse factions within Catholicism and how each thinks about its commitment to Scripture, church, and walking with Christ. A sincere effort to graciously assess the issues that divide, as well as unite, Protestants and Catholics.

—Francis J. Beckwith, author, *Return to Rome: Confessions of an Evangelical Catholic*

Holy Ground is the best tool available for helping former Catholics witness to friends and family members without causing needless offense or compromising the gospel. Castaldo's love for people and firm grasp of biblical principles come through on nearly every page.

—Philip Ryken, Senior Minister, Tenth Presbyterian Church, Philadelphia

I appreciate Castaldo's sensitivity in approaching the differences between Protestants and Catholics. I am certain that engaging, grace-filled dialog will follow from this book, leading Protestants and Catholics to a greater understanding of one another and what they believe.

—Mary Schaller, author, *How to Start a Q Place*

Admirably fair-minded, carefully documented, and pleasantly lucid and irenic—*Holy Ground* will grace the lives and relationships of those Evangelicals with Catholic heritage. An important read for Evangelicals and Catholics alike. Highly recommended.

—R. Kent Hughes, Senior Pastor Emeritus, College Church in Wheaton

HOLY GROUND

WALKING WITH JESUS AS A FORMER CATHOLIC

Chris Castaldo

ZONDERVAN.com/
AUTHORTRACKER
follow your favorite authors

ZONDERVAN

Holy Ground

This title is also available as a Zondervan ebook.
Visit www.zondervan.com/ebooks.

This title is also available in a Zondervan audio edition.
Visit www.zondervan.fm.

Requests for information should be addressed to:

Zondervan, *Grand Rapids, Michigan 49530*

Library of Congress Cataloging-in-Publication Data

Castaldo, Chris, 1971-
Holy ground : walking with Jesus as a former Catholic / Chris Castaldo.
p. cm.
Includes bibliographical references (p. 229) and index.
ISBN 978-0-310-29232-6 (softcover)
1. Catholic Church—Relations—Evangelicalism. 2. Evangelicalism—Relations—Catholic Church. 3. Ex-church members—Catholic Church—Religious life. 4. Protestant converts—Religious life. 5. Castaldo, Chris, 1971- I. Title.
BR1641.C37C35 2010
248.2'44—dc22 2009015941

Interior design by Michelle Espinoza

Printed in the United States of America

10 11 12 13 14 15 • 23 22 21 20 19 18 17 16 15 14 13 12 11 10 9 8 7 6 5 4

This book is dedicated to
my parents, Al and Judy Castaldo,
and my in-laws, John and Susan Bixby

CONTENTS

PREFACE

We have free-floating guilt, can identify the Ave Maria within three notes, and likely have rosary beads somewhere in the attic. We also own at least one study Bible, listen to sermons in the car, and know that a "quiet time" is different from a nap.

We are followers of Christ who grew up Roman Catholic and are now Evangelical Protestants.

We wrestle with a series of challenges. Religious guilt still nips at our heels, and Christmas dinner at your brother Philip's house (the one who is the Grand Poo-bah of the Knights of Columbus) is more than a little awkward. We were simply trying to give thanks before eating our meal, and for some reason Aunt Louise is now compelled to recite the Hail Mary. It's going to be a long night!

Some of us walked with Jesus as Catholics before we moved in an Evangelical direction. Others of us were converted to Christ as we made the move. Either way, our ambition is simple. We want to live for Jesus Christ by embodying his grace and winsomely sharing it with Catholic friends and loved ones. And this is where the challenge begins.

Through an extended narrative describing my personal journey as a devout Catholic who worked with bishops and priests before eventually becoming an Evangelical pastor, I seek to help readers understand the following:

- the priorities which drive Catholic faith and practice.
- where the lines of continuity and discontinuity fall between Catholicism and Evangelicalism.

- the delicate dynamics that make up our relationships.
- some principles for lovingly sharing the gospel of salvation by grace alone.
- a historical overview of Catholicism from the Reformation to the present.

In treating these topics, my hope is that *Holy Ground* differs from other books on this subject in two ways.

First, books by Evangelicals which address Catholicism often convey an unkind attitude. The doctrinal emphasis of these works is commendable, but the irritable tone rings hollow and fails to exhibit the loving character of Jesus. It's the tone that my seminary professor warned against when he said, "Don't preach and write as though you have just swallowed embalming fluid. As Christ imparts redemptive life, so should his followers." This life is communicated in the content of God's message and *also* in its manner of presentation. Therefore, we seek to express genuine courtesy toward Catholics, even in disagreement.

Second, most books on Roman Catholicism and Evangelicalism emphasize doctrinal tenets without exploring the practical dimensions of personal faith. However, there's often a vast difference between the content of catechisms and the beliefs of folks who fill our pews. This book is concerned with understanding the common ideas and experiences of real-life people.

Through years of research, I've interviewed all kinds of Catholics and Evangelicals in focus groups to learn about their most pressing questions and concerns. Thanks to their candid feedback, I've uncovered a wide range of insights. I've also used a web-based survey which has expanded the scope of our study to include anyone with internet access.

Based on those responses, I've decided to address two basic needs which regularly surfaced in conversation. These needs are taken up in the two overarching sections of the book. In part 1, I'll discuss the five major reasons why followers of Christ often leave the Catholic Church, while touching on key figures from church history who elucidate these reasons. Part 2 is concerned with how to naturally and winsomely emulate Jesus among our Catholic loved ones and friends.

One issue deserving comment is our choice of the word *Evangelical*. It has become one of those slippery words that defy easy definition. Given a host of factors such as time period, locale, cultural forms, and the influence of media upon public perception, to say nothing of genuine doctrinal differences, we could devote the remainder of this book to the question of definition and still fall short. For the purposes of this book, I will instead point readers to a historically respected statement of faith: the Lausanne Covenant, drafted in 1974. Because Lausanne drew Christian leaders from around the world, it has the advantage of representing an international range of thought. The combined input from non-Western scholars and practitioners makes it well-rounded, substantive, and readable. You may access the document on the Lausanne website: *www.lausanne.org*.

■■■

Because our subject is as familiar to me as the home in which I grew from infancy into adulthood, writing this book has been especially tough. It's generally easier to address topics one doesn't know very well. There are fewer uncertainties, fewer grey hues to blend, more black-and-white lines. But for me, growing up as a member of the Catholic Church and working full-time in it, I have had years of firsthand experience. I have participated in many Masses, much banter over coffee with priest friends in parish rectories, and many rounds of golf in which Father so-and-so graciously walked with me through the tall grass looking for my lost ball (while his ball was on the green).

Yet more than familiarity with the subject, the toughest element of writing has been the nature of the topic—describing how former Catholics walk with Jesus. He is a fool who engages such a topic without fear and trembling. Then one must double-, triple-, and quadruple-check the details of his argument and, of equal importance, the attitude and tone with which they are expressed. This awareness of one's limitations and our requisite dependence upon divine grace is what has given rise to the title *Holy Ground*. It is where we live, with humility before the throne of God, full of inadequacies and yet trusting in God's mercy. It was in this lowly spirit, motivated by a desire to elevate Christ, that the book was written, and hopefully it will also characterize the way it is applied.

Finally, I'll say a word about what you will encounter in the following pages. They contain several intertwining stories, including stories of brokenness: broken assumptions, broken expectations, and broken traditions. Yet it also contains stories of redemption: redeemed faith, redeemed hope, and redeemed relationships. If you're a former Catholic, these stories are yours.

ACKNOWLEDGMENTS

High-octane energy and sobering fear are a lively combination. As a first-time author, I've known much of this mixture. Some days the energy has made me feel as though I could hug a man-sized tree and rip it from the ground, roots and all. Other days, when the fear quotient rose, I have wanted to stay in bed in a fetal position and suck my thumb. In both instances, God has exercised sovereign oversight in the most curious and confounding ways. Usually he did so through others. These are the people I would like to thank. Without them, this book would have remained nothing more than a collection of notes in my file cabinet.

Kent Hughes, my friend and former pastor, thanks for planting the seed; David Cook, thanks for inspiring me to think as only an Oxford don can; and Harold Smith, thanks for your one sentence that improved my writing.

Wendell Hawley, thanks for taking me under your wing. Steve Board, I won't know how much you've helped until heaven. Alan Youngren, my agent, your savvy is only exceeded by your sense of humor. I look forward to more laughs over coffee.

Dan Meyer, thanks for making it possible for me to sing the Ave Maureena.

Thanks to my editors, Andy Meisenheimer, for believing in this title from the start and making it better than it was, and Brian Phipps, for your punctilious scrutiny.

To the congregation and elders of College Church in Wheaton, thanks for the privilege of letting me serve as one of your pastors.

To my colleagues at College Church for the joy of partnering with you in the gospel.

To my professors Henri Blocher, Edith Blumhofer, Harry Hoffner, Jon Laansma, Mike McDuffee, and David Wells for providing illumination.

To friends who've offered invaluable feedback on the manuscript: Nina Cunningham, Joan Engeseth, Caleb Evans, Peter Feuerherd, Timothy George, Stan Guthrie, Ralph MacKenzie, Sarah Miglio, and Linda Schuch.

To my buddies, whose shoulders have always been available to lean on: Pete Figliozzi, Paul Adams, Mark Brucato, Chris Blumhofer, Collin Hansen, Doug O'Donnell, and Nathanael Szobody.

To the former Catholics who participated in our focus groups and interviews, thanks for your candor.

To my parents, Al and Judy, sister, Jeanette, and Nana Jean for your enduring love and support.

To my boys, Luke, Philip, and Simeon for sharing Daddy.

To my dear wife, Angelina, for challenging me to think, for supporting my tired arms, and for enriching all of life with your sweet love.

Finally, to the triune God—Father, Son, and Holy Spirit—for your redemptive grace, which enlivens dry bones and makes them dance; to you alone be all glory and honor forever.

PROLOGUE

IT'S ONLY LIFE AND DEATH

I knew I was in trouble when the bishop removed a string of black, shiny rosary beads from his suit pocket. We had just concluded an evening banquet for wealthy donors on St. John's Island in Florida—the kind of donors whose Mercedes and Jaguar sedans were always buffed. As I drove south on Highway 90 to the bishop's home, he announced from the passenger seat his desire for us to pray. Even though I was employed full-time in the Catholic Church, he had reason to believe I was an Evangelical.

How could I—a newly minted Evangelical—pray the rosary?

The bishop suggested that I recite the Our Father while he addressed himself to Mary. Since the Our Father (called the Lord's Prayer by Evangelicals) is in Scripture, I appeased my conscience with a quick rationalization and determined to concentrate on my part of the prayer.

Bishop Symons and I had become friends during the year as we visited parishes together. He spoke on behalf of the diocese, and as the fundraiser, I delivered the motivational speech intended to fill Catholic offering plates with coins. Our dynamic-duo approach had the flavor of an Archbishop Fulton Sheen—the articulate Catholic television preacher from the 1950s—and a young Dale Carnegie salesman making the pitch. Following each presentation, people lined up to kiss his ring and hand me their checks.

While cruising down the highway, I remembered the exhortation my Evangelical pastor had issued to our congregation the previous day: he called it the Sixty-Day Gospel Challenge. We were supposed to share our personal faith in Jesus at least once a day for sixty days. Unfortunately, I had been so engrossed in work that it had slipped my mind.

Suddenly an idea emerged: I could share my faith with the bishop. But how does a young Evangelical Christian witness to a gray-haired Catholic bishop? What could I possibly say? After a moment's reflection, I decided to tell my conversion story. It was long overdue.

With my heart racing and whitened knuckles gripping the steering wheel, I took a deep breath and explained how divine mercy had invaded my life. For fifteen minutes, I tried to explain my encounter with God, describing how Jesus' death and resurrection connected my empty heart with saving grace. All the while, I stared intently at the road before me, afraid to make eye contact. Sweat forming on my forehead, I finally reached the conclusion of my monolog.

And—there was silence! The bishop said nothing. My fear became dread as I anticipated the blast of an anathematizing canon.

When I could no longer bear the quietness, I slowly turned toward the passenger seat. The bishop was also looking straight at the windshield. Noticing his eyes were closed, I assumed he was collecting his thoughts, but then I heard his heavy breathing.

The bishop was fast asleep!

OUR CHALLENGE

My attempt to talk with the bishop about Christian faith expresses the struggle of many who leave the Roman Catholic Church. You might say the challenge is twofold. First, we wrestle to understand how our Catholic background influences our view of God and his church. Second, we struggle with how to relate the gospel to Catholic friends and loved ones.

In regard to the first, when Catholics become Evangelical, we quickly realize that our walk with Jesus has been shaped by our religious background. For instance, perhaps the most common and spiritually injurious issue is the problem of unhealthy religious guilt. It's a nagging fear that preoccupies the soul, a root of doubt that questions whether we are truly forgiven in Christ. In bed at night I often wondered, "Has my behavior been good enough to merit divine approval?" Like Martin Luther, who attempted to find a gracious God, I never knew whether I had successfully produced a sufficient amount of righteousness.

Throughout his writings, Martin Luther describes his struggle to please God with the German word *Anfechtung*. English lacks an adequate translation. In Luther's day it communicated a severe torment of soul and conscience. It's perhaps best to let Luther describe it. About his days in the Catholic monastery, he writes, "I was a devout monk and wanted to force God to justify me because of my works and the severity of my life. I was a good monk, and kept the rule of my order so strictly that I may say that if ever a monk got to heaven by his monkery, I would have gotten there as well. All my brothers in the monastery who knew me will bear me out. If I had kept on any longer, I would have killed myself with vigils, prayers, reading, and other works."[1]

In subsequent chapters we'll learn how Luther's soul realized divine liberation from his angst and consider how we may obtain the same.

The second struggle occurs when we relate to Roman Catholic friends and family. As an Evangelical pastor, I commonly find these relational breakdowns unfolding in our community: a married couple, one of whom is Evangelical and the other a Catholic, must decide which church they will attend. Do the children join youth group or their parish's equivalent? How about fulfilling sacraments like Holy Communion? Is it okay for Evangelical parents to approve of their children's observance of Catholic customs with which they disagree?

---

1. Walther von Loewenich, *Martin Luther: The Man and His Work*, trans. Lawrence E. Denef (Minneapolis: Augsburg, 1982), 72.

Do such concessions communicate loving support or a negligent compromise? These issues often tear the fabric of marriage and family.

In addition to problems that occur within one's immediate family, there are also difficulties with extended relatives. For instance, Grandma Amelia dies and her family must decide if she is to have a Mass or an Evangelical funeral. Do you put a cross or a crucifix over her casket? Is it okay to sing the Ave Maria? These may sound like insignificant questions; however, families regularly face them, with precious relationships hanging in the balance.

The issue of Evangelical-Catholic relations not only is pressing on families but also has profound implications for large numbers of people, not least of which is the hurting world, which needs to see the life of Christ. Consider this story: Lord James Mackay was born in Edinburgh, Scotland, in 1927, into an extremely devout Evangelical family that belonged to the Free Presbyterian Church. It was there that young Mackay was raised to love Christ. His devotion was evidenced by his thirty years of service as a church elder. In his distinguished career as England's most eminent judge, Mackay's reputation for being a man of faith preceded him.

The problem started when two of Mackay's colleagues died, both of whom happened to be Roman Catholic. After attending the second of these funeral services, Lord Mackay was confronted by Free Presbyterian Church elders. They accused him of sin, asserting that the Catholic funeral services he attended included Masses, which they considered to be an affront to the gospel of Scripture. The charge was not that Mackay had taken the Eucharist but that he had simply attended the services. Consequently, he was not permitted to serve or to take Communion in his denomination until he repented. When he defended his actions, the case was reviewed by the synod. A vote was taken and went against him, thirty-three to twenty-seven. In the aftermath of his censuring, Lord Mackay left the Free Presbyterian Church.

The decision of the synod to discipline Mackay for attending the Catholic funerals was so intensely controversial that the issue divided

Free Presbyterians throughout Scotland. Many spoke out on behalf of Mackay, and when they didn't receive a hearing, entire congregations broke off to form another denomination. They created what eventually came to be called Associated Presbyterian Churches. The interesting twist is that when these churches seceded, a legal battle ensued over the ownership of their church buildings. Who would get the parish land and facilities? Did they belong to the congregation or the denomination? The disagreement was so sharply disputed that it ascended to the highest court in the United Kingdom—the courtroom of none other than Lord Chancellor James Mackay.

THE OPPORTUNITY BEFORE US

The Tiber River is among the longest rivers in Italy, flowing some 406 kilometers down from the Tuscan mountains through the city of Rome. It winds through the old city like a serpent, flowing beneath an intricate network of bridges. One such overpass is the Ponte Vittorio. Heading north over the bridge, one eventually reaches the famous Via della Conciliazione (the Way of Conciliation), the primary access route to the Vatican. A sharp turn and there in front of you is the breathtaking Basilica of St. Peter, where the embracing arms of the Bernini Colonnade reach out to enfold you.

As tourists travel into the Vatican, it is easy to miss the beauty and wonder of the Tiber. After all, it's just a river, and Bernini's architecture is impressive. However, if one were to step onto a boat and travel west on the river, things would look vastly different. Leaving from Ponte Sant'Angelo dock, the Tiber accompanies you into the heart of the city. Enormous trees line the river banks and suddenly clear to provide magnificent views of the Eternal City and eventually of the Vatican itself.

Because the river runs directly beside Vatican City, it is sometimes used to describe one's relationship to the Roman Catholic Church. Thus, "swimming the Tiber" is shorthand for one's conversion to Catholicism. I'd like to suggest that it also says something about how Catholics and Evangelicals relate.

Sometimes the river is calm and placid; often, though, it threatens travelers with whitewater. People who have vacationed on a Tiber riverboat can testify that the voyage is preceded by great anticipation and the promise of lifelong memories. As the boat floats past the Vatican, with the dome of St. Peter's glistening in the sun, camera shutters click and drinking glasses clink while passengers give little thought to the sharp stones sitting below the surface. Thanks to the captain's skill, they navigate safely around danger.

Similarly, we approach gatherings with Catholics full of hope. Whatever the occasion, a holiday or weekly luncheon, the opportunity to relish friendship awaits us. However, like passengers on a cruise, we are sometimes unaware that lurking below the surface of relationships are jagged differences of belief which terrorize their vitality.

As one whose life has been spent floating down both sides of the Tiber, this is a portrait of how I moved from Catholic belief to serving as an Evangelical pastor. Along the way, I've scraped against more than a few stones, each of which represents a lesson. The following pages explore these lessons, intended to encourage you in your pursuit of Jesus.

A pastoral colleague of mine used to say that "it's just a matter of life or death, nothing more, nothing less."[2] Hanging in the balance are relationships which can either highlight the beauty of Christ's redemption or degenerate into a self-serving waste of time. The former has implications which affect eternity; the latter is nothing more than hollow vanity. This is what makes the need for these lessons so vital.

2.This is one of many lines I've picked up from my former colleague Kent Hughes.

Part 1

PERSPECTIVES ON ROMAN CATHOLICISM

Chapter 1

UNDERSTANDING WHY CATHOLICS BECOME EVANGELICAL

I grew up a good Catholic boy in St. Joseph's Parish on Long Island.[1] The cobblestone walkway to the church entrance was lined with dense clusters of yellow daffodils. Both hands were required to pull open the gigantic oak doors. Upon entering, one was greeted by a russet brick facade, flanked by truncated Gothic arches. The panorama of banners and statuary conveyed a rich history which infused the soul with a joyful gravity. Carved wooden pews appeared to have the posture of an army standing at attention before its general. As a young boy, I wondered, "Am I an enemy standing on foreign territory, or do I belong here?"

I remember on one occasion walking through an amber glow which filtered through the rose glass window. Tiny lint particles floated through rays of light to display a kaleidoscope of color. As these dust clouds slowly ascended and celestial beams shone down, a picture of divine redemption appeared. Humans are dust; God is light.

---

1. In some conversations and events, names and minor details have been modified for privacy and clarity. When taking this literary license, I have been careful to preserve the meaning and overall accuracy of each story.

However, when the beauty of God's presence shines on us, shadowy pieces of earth are beckoned upward to reflect the reality of heaven. My Catholic parish offered many such lessons.

Early church memories among Catholics often consist of votive candles, patent-leather Easter shoes, Christmas pageants, and flannelgraphs. Mine are not so religious. My chief memory has to do with entering church during winter. Running into the parish from the frosty tundra of a parking lot, most children passed quickly through the foyer to find warmth in the nave. I learned, however, that the defrosting process could be hastened by surreptitiously dipping both of my hands in the font of lukewarm holy water. It only took a few seconds of immersion before sensation was restored. It worked well.

Unfortunately, I once performed this trick when Father Tom was standing directly behind me. He spoke my name in his deep, commanding voice. Frightened, I spun around, flicked the water from my fingers onto his white cassock, and without missing a beat, sheepishly responded, "Bless you, Father," before running away. Years later, he shared the story in a homily as the funniest experience of his vocation and mentioned that he forgot which lad it was. For this lapse of memory I was relieved, but at the time, I envisioned the flames of purgatory.

CONFRONTED BY DEATH

When I was nine, my paternal grandfather died suddenly. It happened on a sunny afternoon when he and my grandmother were at Belmont Racetrack, just outside New York City. After the third race, Grandpa rushed through the crowded walkway to place another bet. While standing in line, he suddenly dropped dead from a heart attack. After an hour of anxious waiting, Grandma left her seat to learn the news.

The following Sunday morning, I sat in church with a flood of questions in my head. It was the first time I thought seriously about death. In my nine-year-old mind, I wondered, "Where is Grandpa today? Is he in heaven? If so, what is he doing? Maybe he's in purgatory. What should I do to help him? Pray the rosary? Go to Mass?" My questions weren't articulated so clearly. Nevertheless, I wondered.

Later in the week I attended my weekly Confraternity of Christian Doctrine (CCD) class, where I questioned our teacher, Mrs. Fiero, about it. When she learned of my grandfather's death, she asked one of the parish deacons to talk with me personally.

Joe Lorenzo had been a deacon for many years. He stood about five foot eight and weighed almost two hundred and fifty pounds. His smile was so big and bright that it filled the room. Big Joe (as kids secretly called him) spoke briefly with Mrs. Fiero before he invited me to take a walk with him. Just outside of our classroom and down the hall was the parish sanctuary, where Joe and I sat in a rear pew. I have a vague recollection of the dialog. It went something like the following.

"Chris, look up at the wall. What do you see?"

"A station of the cross."

"Yes, station number 13 in fact. Jesus is being taken down from the cross with Mary embracing his lifeless body. You don't have to look at it for very long before you begin to feel something of our holy Mother's sorrow.

"Despite the modesty of the crucifix, which features Jesus in a loin cloth, we know that crucified men actually hung beaten and unclothed: an unspeakable disgrace to Jews, and especially so for the Jewish mother for whom the circumcision of her son was the most joyous day of her life. Our blessed Mother's soul magnified the Lord at his birth; now at his death, she suffers in his pain.

"Thankfully, Chris, this is only the second-to-last station. The final depiction of our Lord's passion, station 14, portrays Jesus lying in the tomb. The tomb is a symbol of death, but it also signifies hope—that one day life will flourish."

Joe's eyes turned to a nearby window. "Let's continue to talk outside."

WHAT DO CATHOLICS BELIEVE?

As we headed out together, the dim sanctuary was quickly contrasted by the bright world beyond the large wooden doors. The sunlight was blinding, so much so that for a few moments all I could see was a silhouette of Big Joe before me. The redbrick path outside the doors veered off to an outcropping of flowers, bushes, and fruit trees. At the end of the brick path was a wooden bench where we eventually sat.

Joe initially was quiet as he stared up at the cherry tree in front of us, on top of the woodchip mound.

"Chris, have you ever considered how barren trees look in winter? Branches appear naked and dead, but in fact, life is hidden within. It's in springtime when what's concealed is revealed.

"Look for instance at this cherry tree. It is now beginning to break from dormancy. You'll notice the fragrant white flowers are beginning to bud on the ends of the branches. This is the first step in what will eventually become a cluster of black cherries.

"What do you suppose would happen to this flower if I pulled it off the branch?"

"Death."

"Precisely. Unless the flower remains connected, it can't live. You know, your grandpa was baptized into the church. His faith was nurtured by the sacraments. On account of this, we hope that his life will blossom again."

I looked at the ground, plucked a dandelion, and asked, "So, like, the church is the tree?"

With one of his jovial smiles, Joe responded, "Yes."

"How does it work?"

"It starts with God, the Creator of all things. Each Sunday when we celebrate the Mass, we express this in the Gloria in Excelsis. It is a beautiful hymn of praise which dates back to the fourth century:

You alone are the Holy One
You alone are the Lord,
You alone are the Most High, Jesus Christ
with the Holy Spirit,
to the glory of God the Father. Amen.

"The second member of the triune God became a man, Jesus the God-man, as it says in the Nicene Creed:

> *We believe in one Lord, Jesus Christ, the only Son of God,*
> *eternally begotten of the Father,*
> *God from God, Light from Light, true God from true God,*
> *begotten, not made, one in Being with the Father.*
> *Through him all things were made.*
> *For us men and for our salvation he came down from heaven ...*

"Jesus selected twelve men to be his closest disciples. He gave them authority and called them to proclaim the good news of God's kingdom. This is why we call them 'the apostles,' because they were sent to serve as ambassadors of Christ to the world.

"Representing the tribes of Israel, the twelve apostles united under Jesus Christ in a divine mission. Among them, Simon Peter received the primary role of spokesman and leader. The Lord bestowed his authority upon Peter for this purpose, as Matthew's gospel tells us: 'And I tell you, you are Peter, and on this rock I will build my church, and the gates of hell shall not prevail against it. I will give you the keys of the kingdom of heaven, and whatever you bind on earth shall be bound in heaven, and whatever you loose on earth shall be loosed in heaven.'[2]

"Peter was the first pope. His pastoral office is continued by a succession of popes down through history. As the vicar [representative] of Christ, the pope serves as the Roman pontiff and leads the bishops in exercising supreme power over the universal church. Together, they grant access to God."[3]

"Joe, forgive me, but how does all this relate to our tree?"

---

2. Matt. 16:18–19.

3. For a precise explanation of how apostolic succession is thought to work, see Pope Benedict's chapter "The Key Question in *The Catholic-Protestant Dispute: Tradition and Successio Apostolica*," in Joseph Cardinal Ratzinger, *Principles of Catholic Theology: Building Stones for Fundamental Theology*, trans. Sr. Mary Frances McCarthy, S.N.D. (San Francisco: Ignatius, 1987), 239–84.

Joe cracked another warm smile and continued, "Imagine the church as the tree and Catholic people as the flowers. Just as sap flows to the far reaches of every branch, God's grace is infused to every member of the church. As we remain connected to the tree, divine life is deposited into our souls. This is why the Eucharist is so vital; it provides spiritual nourishment."

"How does the church deposit life into our souls?"

"The exact way the sacraments work is a mystery of faith, but we can rely on them just the same because they have been instituted by God.[4] Through them we receive the life of Jesus."

Before Big Joe continued, the school bell rang, indicating that class was finished. In unison we looked to the church building, where children were starting to exit. After I thanked Joe for his time, he pronounced a blessing over me and we went our separate ways. At the time, I may not have understood all that Joe said, but I knew without question that it came from a man who cared deeply for my soul.

THE FUNDAMENTAL DIFFERENCE

Those of us who are Evangelical will find in Joe's explanation doctrinal elements that are familiar and others that are perhaps foreign. In the upcoming chapters we will clarify many of these details, but for now, I want to identify the fundamental difference between Catholic and Evangelical belief.

Like two sets of dominos that run parallel before moving in divergent directions, the Catholic and Evangelical understandings of Christ and salvation both emerge from a common Bible[5] and creedal

4. *Catechism of the Catholic Church*, para. 775, ed. 2 (Citta del Vatticano: Libreria Editrice Vaticana, 1997).

5. Notwithstanding the so-called Old Testament apocrypha, or in Catholic terms the "deuterocanonicals." These are a collection of writings found in the Catholic Old Testament from the intertestamental period (the four hundred years between the Old and New Testaments) comprising seven books: Tobit, Judith, 1 Maccabees, 2 Maccabees, Wisdom of Solomon, Sirach (also called Ecclesiasticus), and Baruch. In addition, there are also passages of text: the Letter to Jeremiah (which became Baruch chap. 6), the Prayer of Azariah (which became Dan. 3:24–90), an additional 107 verses on the Book of Esther, Susanna

confessions (for example, the Apostles' Creed and the Nicene Creed) but thereafter begin to separate. The cause of this divergence comes down to a different interpretation of how the revelation and authority of Jesus extends to his church, and by extension into the world. As Deacon Joe explained, Catholics understand the incarnated presence of Jesus to be in the one, holy, catholic, and apostolic church. This is why the church is thought to have divine authority over God's people.[6] Evangelicals agree with this connection to the extent that we recognize the church as the body of Christ. At the same time, there are significant points at which we disagree.

Unlike the Catholic position, which is based upon apostolic succession, Evangelicals understand Jesus' infallible revelation to consist of Scripture alone. A simple way to think of it is the correlation between Jesus the *living* Word, and Jesus the *written* Word. As the start of John's gospel puts it, "In the beginning was the Word, and the Word was with God, and the Word was God" (John 1:1; see also 1 John 1:1). Accordingly, Scripture is the way in which Jesus' risen life extends to the church. Through the sacred text, God grants new life,[7] reveals his will,[8] and rules over his people.[9] The Bible is the sole infallible guide for salvation. It stands alone as the supreme source of authority upon which Christian faith is based, the absolute "norm that sets the norm" (*norma normans*).[10] This is different from the Catholic view, which understands Sacred Tradition to be equally authoritative as Scripture.[11]

(which became Daniel 13), and Bel and the Dragon (which became Daniel 14). These books were made an official part of the Catholic Old Testament at the Council of Trent (1545–63).

6. Sebastian Tromp, SJ, *Corpus Christi quaod est ecclesia*, trans. Ann Condit (New York: Vantage, 1960), 194.
7. John 5:24; Rom. 10:8–10; Eph. 1:13; James 1:18 (compare with Heb. 4:12).
8. Matt. 4:4; 7:21; 1 Tim. 3:6–16; 2 Tim. 2:15; 3:16–17; Heb. 1:2.
9. John 17:17; 1 Cor. 14:37; Phil. 2:16; 1 Tim. 5:17.
10. Acts 17:11; 1 Cor. 3:11; 1 Thess. 2:13; Harold O. J. Brown, *Reclaiming the Great Tradition*, ed. James S. Cutsinger (Downers Grove, IL: InterVarsity, 1997), 79.
11. *Catechism of the Catholic Church*, para. 97.

With this basic point of divergence in mind, we can better understand why Catholics and Evangelicals differ.[12] In a single word, it comes down to a difference of "authority."

Most of the former Catholics who completed our survey pointed to the issue of religious authority as the reason for moving in an Evangelical direction. As our questionnaires and focus groups unpacked this concern, five issues rose to the top. With authority as their common thread, these convictions constitute the particular reasons why individuals eventually departed from their Catholic backgrounds:

1. Every believer is called to full-time ministry.
2. Relationship with Christ must take precedence over rules-keeping.
3. We enjoy direct access to God in Christ.
4. There is only one proper object of devotion—Jesus the Savior.
5. God's children should be motivated by grace instead of guilt.

After numerous interviews in living rooms with a dozen or so people over coffee and biscotti, I realized something fascinating. Former Catholics enjoy hearing one another's stories of faith because such stories offer insight into one's own spiritual journey. These personal accounts provide answers to important questions and supply evidence to support the aformentioned thesis concerning the convictions that drive individuals from the Catholic Church. The following chapters explore the most commonly mentioned reasons for this departure and present three historical portraits from the Reformation period to further illuminate how such convictions get worked out.

12. Another way to understand the divergence is in terms of "allegiance," as Jaroslav Pelikan puts it in his classic book *The Riddle of Roman Catholicism*. Allegiance to Christ will appear to be different between Catholics and Evangelicals, the former defining it by allegiance to the church institution and the latter in terms of personal faith in Christ (Jaroslav Pelikan, *The Riddle of Roman Catholicism* [Nashville: Abingdon, 1959], 179).

Chapter 2

REASON ONE: FULL-TIME FAITH

The enterprise of developing a popular image is vital to Americans. Whether it drives by on a bus or assaults us through a pop-up window, image anxiety is everywhere. It is especially obvious in shopping malls, which have become places of worship not unlike ancient temples or medieval cathedrals. These modern-day chapels are a sight to behold, with their luxuriant foliage, sparkling fountains, and colorfully illuminated vistas. Along with designer jeans and exotic coffees, you can acquire a new and improved image.[1]

It must be pointed out, however, that concern for one's image is not only for the fashion conscious; it's also vital for the servant of Christ. Along this line, I once wrote an article titled "Christian Image Is Everything." The title raised a few eyebrows among my pastor friends until they read it. I made the case that when the Bible talks about God's image, it is simultaneously concerned with our calling to advance Christ's majesty throughout the earth. In other words, God's image is more than reflecting his moral attributes (holiness, righteousness, love, etc.); it's also our calling to spread his beauty and his fame. In this way, the concept of image has everything to do with God's purpose for our lives.

---

1. I first heard of the shopping mall used as a metaphor to describe popular culture by Professor David F. Wells in a seminary lecture.

EXCURSUS: IMAGE OF GOD

To properly understand the biblical meaning of *image*, we must consider Adam and Eve in the garden. Having been created in God's image, Adam functioned like an angled mirror postured beneath the Lord. As divine reality shone down upon him, it was reflected outward along a horizontal plane. Accordingly, when the newly created couple approached one another, they beheld something of God's glory in each other.

Unfortunately, Adam and Eve rebelled against the Creator, and as fruit juice dripped from their lips, the divine image was shattered. Unable to reflect divine beauty with the same degree of clarity, they were expelled from the garden. This legacy of disgrace is our birthright.

With a shameful heritage of sin and death, the human race, now separated from God, tries desperately to restore its shattered image by accumulating the trappings of the world. We pursue everything that promises wholeness: money, leisure, sex, power, fashion, corporate promotions. Sadly, many people reach the end of their lives surrounded by these hollow emblems, only to find that the promise of prosperity and personal satisfaction was a sham. Here, in a culture haunted by fragmentation, hi-tech distractedness, and the loneliness of individualism, our hearts remain empty theaters of longing. Thankfully, God doesn't leave us to die in this deception. Jesus, the visible image of God's glory—the pristine mirror who remained postured faithfully beneath the Father—has decisively addressed humanity's problem.

The apostle Paul says, "He [Christ] is the image of the invisible God" (Col. 1:15). As a substitute for humanity, the sacrificial love of Christ conformed to the cross. On it, the Savior was pierced by nails of divine judgment. Just as it had been planned from before the beginning of time, he became the Lamb of God who takes away the sin of the world, the Savior who makes all things new.

The death and resurrection of Christ have direct bearing on humanity's image problem. On account of Jesus' resurrection from the dead, God not only justified us; he also called us to represent him in the world (Matt. 28:19–20). This is the enduring purpose of God's people, the image of Christ which we now reflect.

We all feel some responsibility to grasp life's purpose. It's a rare person indeed who doesn't arise from the pillow in the morning and occasionally wonder, *What's it all about?* Or maybe it comes while looking at the funeral casket of a loved one. The question of purpose is critical for everyone who has a pulse, to say nothing of those who believe that the unexamined life is not worth living. During my teen age years, concern for image and purpose not only loomed large; it also marked the beginning of my departure from the Catholic Church.

SEARCHING FOR PURPOSE

The fast pace of life through the 1970s shuffled the priorities of our family. Even though I completed the sacrament of confirmation, our parish participation was eventually reduced to holidays. As years passed, we unintentionally joined the ranks of those whose Catholicism consisted of attending Mass on Christmas and Easter—so-called Chreasters.

One of the few places where my Catholic identity became explicit was in the hospital. You may know how this goes. The clerk asks you to identify your religious affiliation at the emergency room entrance. In the hospital trade on the north shore of Long Island, this kind of information can be very important, lest, for instance, patient Murray Rabinowitz find himself staring at a pork tenderloin sandwich. I told the clerk, "Roman Catholic."

When I was nineteen, living at home on Long Island, a mysterious illness landed me in the hospital. Breathing was difficult, and a strange rash appeared on my palms. After being admitted, I was greeted by a rotation of doctors who shuffled through my room asking diagnostic questions. After several hours of seeing bewildered expressions, I was moved to a quarantine area where all visitors were required to wear medical face masks. The panic in everyone's eyes was noticeable.

A nurse mentioned that my labored breathing was because of an influx of fluid which was filling my lungs.

I responded, "Excuse me, but how do we remove the fluid?"

"Antibiotics," she said, while replacing my empty IV bag. "And if that doesn't work, we extract it."

"Extract it?"

"Yes, it's quite simple. We insert a needle through your lower back and push it deep into your lungs while you force out the fluid with deep breaths. Oh well, there's no point explaining it all now. We'll cross that bridge when we reach it."

I looked for the nurse's smile, hoping it was a joke, but none came. Feeling nervous, I gazed through my second-story window at a branch which had lost nearly all of its leaves to the winter wind. My mind went to the picture of Jesus' sacred heart hanging behind my bedroom door.

The time of my convalescence raised profound questions about life's meaning. Why was I alive? Is there really a God, and if so, does he care to be involved in my life? With each day, questions grew and eventually settled into a resolution to find answers. On that cold winter day when the young nurse rolled my wheelchair through the exit doors of the hospital, my spiritual quest was underway.

The first step of my quest was to pursue transcendental meditation with the Maharishi Mahesh Yogi. After a few months of making unusual noises in a lotus position, I understood why the Beatles became disenchanted with Mr. Yogi's method. From there I went on to attend seminars through the Learning Annex, studying under world-class gurus like M. Scott Peck and Deepak Chopra.

I was working with New York Telephone in Manhattan's Greenwich Village at the time, and I was surrounded by the adherents of a broad range of religions and philosophies. The Village became my classroom. For instance, when I wanted to learn from someone in the nearby Buddhist Center, I arranged for a personal meeting. My method for doing this was dubious, though at the time it made sense. After locating the center's phone terminal, I disconnected their cross-connection wires, reported the trouble, took the repair, and rang the Buddhist Center doorbell to be received by a grateful host. Once inside, I found the person to interview, sat beside a wall jack in her office, pretended I was on hold with the central switchboard, and asked questions. As I recall, I think the Buddhist lady even made me a cup of coffee.

The apex of my spiritual journey was a fire walk. It was at New York's Jacob Javits Center, where over a thousand people waited to hear motivational speaker Tony Robbins. After three hours of his encouraging affirmations, neurolinguistic programming, and some New Age meditation, our massive herd shuffled outside into the parking lot, where we were greeted by long stretches of burning coals and embers. According to Robbins, the experience was designed to be a metaphor for overcoming our fears and improving life. Never before had a metaphor looked so hot and harmful!

When the lady ahead of me proceeded to walk across the twelve-foot path of fire, I inhaled deeply. Tony Robbins' wife (who happened to be facilitating my line) put her hand on my shoulder and said, "You can do this!" I noticed that she was wearing shoes and was at least twenty inches from the nearest coal; nevertheless, I stepped forward and walked as quickly as my trembling legs could carry me.

I don't know how it worked; all I can say is that I walked on the fire without getting burned. After I stepped from the coals, someone immediately hosed down my feet with cold water to extinguish any embers that may have been stuck between my toes. There was a celebration afterward, and in good New York fashion, we exchanged stories over schmeared bagels. It was a thrill, yet the bareness of my heart persisted and my journey on the wide road continued.

THE CHURCH'S CALLING

St. Augustine said, "God has formed us for himself, and our hearts are restless until we find our rest in him."[2] I think the reason why Augustine's statement is so popular is because it exposes a universal need of humanity. As the book of Ecclesiastes puts it, "He [God] has also set eternity in the hearts of men" (3:11). Some people may try to ignore eternity, living only in the present, but they never really escape the eternal purpose for which we are created.

As I mentioned in the beginning of this chapter, the calling of Adam, his purpose if you will, was to reflect God's image on the earth (Gen. 1:26; compare with Psalm 8). All of humanity, following from Adam, inherited the same purpose: to represent God to the world. Eventually, Jesus fulfilled this calling in his perfect life, death, and resurrection.[3] Now, in Christ, the church is called to pursue this great task: to joyfully proclaim Christ's glory among the nations.

For the most part, Catholics and Evangelicals agree on this purpose. We both want to represent Christ our King as an embodiment of his redemptive love in the world. Where we differ is on how to do it. The leading edge of Catholicism is its clerical priesthood; Evangelicals, on the other hand, emphasize the "priesthood of all believers." The difference may sound subtle, but its implications are profound. The following quote from the *Catechism of the Catholic Church* helps make the point: "The whole Church is a priestly people. Through Baptism all the faithful share in the priesthood of Christ. This participation is called the 'common priesthood of the faithful.' Based on this common priesthood and ordered to its service, there exists another participation in the mission of Christ: The ministry conferred by the

2. Anyone who quotes anything from the church fathers knows this statement. We Evangelicals like to sometimes pull it out to demonstrate that we are in touch with church history. (We might also dazzle you with Blaise Pascal or Francis of Assisi, but please don't ask us to share any more lest we reveal our ignorance.)
3. Note Paul's reference to Jesus as the "last Adam" in 1 Cor. 15:45 (see also Rom. 5:14–15).

sacrament of Holy Orders, where the task is to serve in the name and in the person of Christ the Head in the midst of the community."[4]

Please note that the Catholic Church does in fact have a doctrine of the "priesthood of believers," which applies to the entire church. However, even after Vatican II, Catholicism still makes a clear distinction between the roles of the clergy and the laity. The clergy are the ordained ministers who mediate sanctifying grace in ways that the laity can't. Consequently, there is a two-tiered structure as it relates to Christian calling and purpose: the clerical tract and the lay tract.

For many, the unfortunate result of such a sharp Catholic clergy-laity distinction is an undermining of Christian calling and purpose. Among ex-Catholics who participated in our focus groups, this issue was regularly mentioned as a key reason why individuals left the Catholic Church. This is not to say that Catholics can't enjoy a lay vocation. Indeed, some do. However, for many, encouragement to engage in ministry was nonexistent.[5]

After reading the Bible's emphasis on the role of *all* people in Christ to advance his kingdom, these former Catholics desired to have their secular vocations validated as legitimate forms of ministry by the church. From Scripture they came to believe that in Christ they are actually spiritual priests whose ministries are on equal footing with ordained clergy.[6]

Dorothy L. Sayers (1893–1957) was an articulate writer and apologist who argued passionately for the relevance of orthodox Christian doctrine as a necessity for living a truly Christian faith. On April 23, 1942, she spoke in Eastbourne, England, about the state of British society during World War II. To rebuild the country's infrastructure,

---

4. *Catechism of the Catholic Church*, para. 1591–92.
5. Vatican II addressed the need for more lay ministry participation in two documents: *Decree on the Apostolate of the Laity* and the *Pastoral Constitution of the Church in the Modern World.* In many parishes, however, the clergy-laity disjunction has continued.
6. In Christ, all believers are priests (Rom. 12:1; Heb. 10:19, 22; 13:15, 16; 1 Peter 2:5, 9) and share in the Lord's kingly reign (1 Cor. 6:2; Eph. 1:3; 2:6; Col. 3:1).

a proper attitude toward work and faith was necessary. As Sayers put it, work and religion could not "become separate departments":

> It is the business of the Church to recognize that the secular vocation, as such, is sacred. Christian people, and particularly perhaps the Christian clergy, must get it firmly into their heads that when a man or woman is called to a particular job of secular work, that is as true a vocation as though he or she were called to specifically religious work.... It is not right for [the church] to acquiesce in the notion that a man's life is divided into the time he spends on his work and the time he spends in serving God. He must be able to serve God in his work, and the work itself must be accepted and respected as the medium of divine creation.
>
> In nothing has the Church so lost her hold on reality as in her failure to understand and respect the secular vocation. She has allowed work and religion to become separate departments, and is astonished to find that, as a result, the secular work of the world is turned to purely selfish and destructive ends, and that the greater part of the world's intelligent workers have become irreligious, or at least, uninterested in religion.
>
> But is it astonishing? *How can any one remain interested in a religion which seems to have no concern with nine-tenths of his life?*[7]

Sayers' last line makes the point. Many former Catholics became disenchanted with a parish that required little of them beyond attending Mass. They craved a calling and purpose they could sink their teeth into outside of Sunday mornings, one that connected with every facet of life. They eventually found it—living as full-time ambassadors of Christ. In this way, restless hearts finally realize God's purpose for humanity.

7. Dorothy L. Sayers, "Why Work?" in *Creed or Chaos?* (New York: Harcourt, Brace, 1949), 56–57, emphasis added.

Chapter 3

A PORTRAIT OF EVANGELICAL FAITH: MARTIN LUTHER

During the time of the Renaissance—the era of Michelangelo, Raphael, Columbus, and Copernicus—many thoughtful Christians agreed that the church needed reform. The papacy's involvement in political affairs often came at the expense of shepherding souls. With Pope Urban ruling from Rome and Clement in Avignon, the Great Papal Schism of an earlier century had introduced a deeper level of bureaucracy. Moving forward into the sixteenth century, political demands continued to compete with spiritual duties.

Some theologians stood in protest against the politicizing trend of the church. In his work *On the Church*, John Wycliffe (1324–84) asserted that one is saved not by his or her church membership but rather by connection to the spiritual body of Christ. This point emphasized the direct relationship of individuals to God over one's activity in the church institution. Following from this emphasis, Wycliffe promoted the translation of the Latin Scriptures into English.

Three generations later, John Hus of Bohemia was inspired by Wycliffe's theology. Unfortunately for Hus, on December 20, 1409, the church issued a decree to eliminate Wycliffism. Immediately, all books by Wycliffe were to be relinquished, his doctrines renounced, and free preaching discontinued wherever it was practiced. When the prohibition was enforced in Bohemia, John Hus became an outlaw. In the year 1412 the archbishop of Prague excommunicated Hus, and on July 6, 1415, Hus was condemned and burned at the stake as a heretic.

By the time 1500 rolled around, the church institution remained largely monolithic, despite a few reforming voices. With the exception of Eastern Orthodox, Jews, and Muslims, virtually everyone in Europe worshiped according to the same Vatican-authorized liturgy. However, in just fifty years, the Protestant Reformation would modify the entire structure of Western Christianity.

MARTIN LUTHER

Although Martin Luther (1483–1546) entered the world during the Renaissance, the town of Mansfeld, Germany, showed little evidence of cultural rebirth during his early years. Because of plagues, thieves, and a folk culture rife with sinister spirits, many people lived in a constant fear of death. European society of this era commonly blended paganism with Christian tradition, creating a fantastically dark Christianity mingled with superstition. In Germany the blowing wind, flowing streams, and tall trees of the forest were thought to be animated by malevolent beings such as elves, fairies, witches, and mermaids. In such an unstable world, spiritual security was a far-fetched dream which eluded many pious Christians. The dream was sometimes artistically portrayed by the Lord Jesus seated on his throne with a lily protruding from one side of his head (symbolizing resurrection) and on the other a sword (representing judgment). Children wondered, "How do I obtain the lily instead of the sword?"

Young Martin demonstrated remarkable energy and intelligence. After completing bachelor's and master's degrees with breakneck speed, he was headed to become a lawyer. However, at age twenty-one he found his career track undergoing a drastic and unexpected change.

The Last Judgment

One day in July of 1505, while walking to law school near the outskirts of a Saxon village, Luther encountered a fierce thunderstorm. Fast-moving clouds sprinkled the parched road on which he traveled, gently at first, and then more intensely. The sky flashed and rumbled before a lightning bolt struck the ground near Luther with a deafening clap. It touched the earth so close to him that it sent him falling to the ground in terror. Exposed to nature's fury, Luther cried out, "Help me, Saint Anne! I will become a monk."

All at once the direction of Luther's life was altered from a career in law to preparing for the priesthood. After six months of examination, followed by a novitiate (a further year of scrutiny), Luther was made a friar and entered the monastery. The ceremony called him to lie prostrate before an altar over a brass plate which covered a tomb. Buried beneath was an Augustinian leader who at the Council in Constance (1415) had condemned John Hus to a martyr's death. As the Augustinian leader's cold body lay in the still, darkness of the tomb, above him the spirit of Wycliffe and Hus beat somewhere in the heart of Luther.

Historian Martin Marty describes the religious passion of Martin Luther by saying, "He makes most sense as a wrestler with God, indeed, as a God-obsessed seeker of certainty and assurance in a time of social trauma and of personal anxiety, beginning with his own."[1] Perhaps Luther remembered the picture of the lily and the sword emanating from Jesus. Regardless, the question of how to please the divine judge burned in his soul. Here Luther candidly describes his experience:

> I greatly longed to understand Paul's Epistle to the Romans and nothing stood in the way but that one expression, "the justice whereby God is just and deals justly in punishing the unjust." My situation was that, although an impeccable monk, I stood before God as a sinner troubled in conscience, and I had no confidence that my merit would assuage him.

1. Martin Marty, *Martin Luther* (New York: Viking Penguin, 2004), xii.

> Night and day I pondered until I saw the connection between the justice of God and the statement that "the just shall live by his faith." Then I grasped that the justice of God is that righteousness by which through grace and sheer mercy God justifies us through faith. Thereupon I felt myself to be reborn and to have gone through open doors into paradise. The whole of Scripture took on a new meaning, and whereas before the "justice of God" had filled me with hate, now it became to me inexpressibly sweet in greater love. This passage of Paul became to me a gate to heaven....
>
> If you have a true faith that Christ is your Savior, then at once you have a gracious God, for faith leads you in and opens up God's heart and will, that you should see pure grace and overflowing love.[2]

As mentioned, Luther's experience is in many ways a prototype for subsequent conversions from Roman Catholicism. Although today's post-Enlightenment, tech-savvy world appears to have advanced light-years beyond the sixteenth century, the same questions about authority and salvation continue to be asked.

Coming to terms with the nature of God's grace changed the trajectory of Luther's life. Historians usually cite October 31, 1517, as the public starting point. It was the day before All Saints Day when Luther posted a sheet of paper on the door of the Castle Church at Wittenberg listing ninety-five theses (propositions) for debate. Chief among his concerns was the sale of indulgences, a practice of the medieval church that promised forgiveness to individuals who performed acts of penance or offered the church a sufficient amount of money (in Luther's day, primarily for the building of St. Peter's Basilica in Rome).[3] Luther's list questioned this practice in provocative ways.

---

2. Roland H. Bainton, *Here I Stand: A Life of Martin Luther* (Nashville: Abingdon, 1978), 49–50.
3. Roman Catholic theology affirms that the guilt of sin can be forgiven only by the blood of Christ. Papal dispensations of forgiveness are thought to cover purgatorial suffering.

Take, for instance, number 82: "Why does not the pope empty purgatory, for the sake of holy love and of the dire need of the souls that are there, if he redeems an infinite number of souls for the sake of miserable money with which to build a Church?"

The pope wasn't particularly flattered or impressed by number 82 (nor by the others for that matter). Luther's theses also addressed the nature of God's grace. Number 62: "The true treasure of the Church is the Most Holy Gospel of the glory and the grace of God."

To our ears Luther's theses may seem reasonable. However, in a day when papal authority controlled Christian discourse (at least in the West), such statements were downright revolutionary. It's like the Chinese student who went toe-to-toe with the armored tank in Tiananmen Square. Onlookers hold their breath and mumble, "What is this maniac doing?" even as they admire his courage.

While Luther's immediate concern was the abuse of indulgences, his larger issue was the extent of church authority. Luther's point was clear. Scripture must have the final word over any other source of authority, including tradition and church councils. It's not surprising that Pope Leo X issued an edict in response to Luther, the title of which was *Exsurge Domine*, so named from the opening words "Arise, O Lord." The introductory sentence reveals the pope's sentiment for Luther. "Arise, O Lord and judge thy cause. A wild boar has invaded thy vineyard. Arise, O Peter. And consider the case of the Holy Roman Church, the mother of all churches. . . ."[4] According to the papal statement, Luther was required to retract his heresies within sixty days or be excommunicated. On December 10, 1520, after the time period had expired, a multitude of Luther's followers and citizens from town gathered at the entranceway to the city dump, where Luther tossed a copy of *Exsurge Domine* into a bonfire. The die was cast. Luther's confrontation with the pope was just a matter of time.

Luther's fateful day came on April 18, 1521. The recently elected Holy Roman Emperor, Charles V, was in Germany to meet with the

---

4. Bainton, *Here I Stand*, 114.

princes through whom he governed the empire. He summoned Luther to the imperial hall in the city of Worms to give an explanation of his teachings. In mid-March the emperor had promised a letter of safe conduct in order for Luther to embark on the journey. Even though friends warned Luther of the danger, on April 2, the Tuesday after Easter, he entered a covered wagon, resolved to make his case.

As Luther rolled through German hamlets, people ran out to greet the man who was risking his life in defiance of the pope. Authorities from some of the towns presented him with honors while common citizens lauded him with praise. In Erfurt, the location of Luther's monastery, the entire university, led by the rector, greeted him at the outskirts of town as they would a prince. Despite the fact that he acquired a severe intestinal infection, he stopped along the way to preach in churches. News of Luther's triumphal procession eventually reached church officials in Worms and created more than a little stir. In the meantime, they could do nothing but await his arrival.

Midmorning of Tuesday, April 16, while town residents were approaching lunch, a herald wearing an eagle upon his cloak trumpeted Luther's imminent appearance. Within moments a flood of citizens and noblemen numbering nearly two thousand persons crowded around the wagon, so much so that the wheels could roll forward at only a snail's pace. The long journey had finally concluded, but the turning of history was about to begin.[5]

Luther understood what was at stake. He mentioned to a friend in advance, "Unless I am restrained by force or the emperor rescinds his invitation, I will enter Worms under the banner of Christ against the gates of hell.... I have had my Palm Sunday. Is all this pomp merely a temptation or is it also a sign of the passion to come?"[6] In just over twenty-four hours Luther received the answer to his question.

Shortly after arriving, Luther was informed that he was to appear before the emperor at 4:00 p.m. on Wednesday, April 17. At the

---

5. Ibid.

6. James M. Kittelson, *Luther the Reformer: The Story of the Man and His Career* (Minneapolis: Augsburg, 1986), 160.

appointed time he was personally escorted to the Bishop's Court, where he was required to wait for two hours before he was summoned into the emperor's presence.

Two questions were directed at Luther. Since the emperor didn't speak German, they were first spoken in Latin. Pointing to about twenty volumes, Dr. Johann von der Ecken asked, "Do you acknowledge [having written] these books lying here?" and "Are you prepared to retract them as a whole or in part?"[7] Before Luther could respond, his lawyer, Hieronymus Schurff, objected, "Let the titles of the books be read!"[8] Luther was taken aback. He had come expecting a debate but now realized that his judges had made their decision and were depriving him of the opportunity to make his case. Luther's response was barely audible: "The books are all mine and I have written more."[9] All eyes of the grand assembly then fixed upon him in a moment of hushed silence to hear if he would go so far as to recant. It appeared that Luther's confidence had wavered; he couldn't offer a clear reply. In tones so subdued that they could hardly be heard, he asked for time to consider the matter. After a brief consultation the assembly reluctantly granted his request. He would have a day to consider the question with the provision that he give a direct answer.

That evening Luther remained in his quarters alone, weighed down by anxiety and doubt. He wrote, "So long as Christ is merciful, I will not recant a single jot or tittle."[10] With nothing but the Word of God to sustain him, the dark night of Luther's soul was underway.

The next day, Luther returned to a larger and more crowded hall. Civil business at the Diet pushed the timing back so that it was nightfall when Luther eventually was summoned. At such a late hour the auditorium was dark, illumined only by candles and smoking torches.

7. Walther von Loewenich, *Martin Luther: The Man and His Work* (Minneapolis: Augsburg, 1986), 193.

8. Ibid.

9. Kittelson, *Luther the Reformer*, 160.

10. Ibid., 161.

He was asked the same questions as the preceding day: did he acknowledge authorship of these books? And would he recant the errors which they contained?

Luther's examiner began with a harsh rebuke:

> His Imperial Majesty has assigned this time to you, Martin Luther, to answer for the books which you yesterday openly acknowledged to be yours. You asked time to deliberate on the question whether you would take back part of what you had said or would stand by all of it. You did not deserve this respite, which has now come to an end, for you knew long before why you were summoned. And everyone—especially a professor of theology—ought to be so certain of his faith that whenever questioned about it he can give a sure and positive answer. Now at last reply to the demand of his Majesty, whose clemency you have experienced in obtaining time to deliberate. Do you wish to defend all of your books or to retract part of them?[11]

Unlike the previous occasion, Luther's response was clear and bold. He opened by apologizing in case he failed to address dignitaries by their proper titles, since his life had been spent in a monk's residence and not in royal courts. He then offered a lengthy speech in which he separated his writings into different categories. When the examiner realized that Luther was trying to create a debate and was not answering the questions directly, he interjected with an aggravated demand: "Luther, you have not answered to the point. You ought not to call in question what has been decided and condemned by councils. Therefore I beg you to give a simple, unsophisticated answer without horns [without deception]. Will you recant or not?"[12]

11. Clyde L. Manschreck, ed., "The Church from the Reformation to the Present," in vol. 2 of *A History of Christianity: Readings in the History of the Church* (Grand Rapids, MI: Baker, 1981), 29–30.

12. Ibid., 31.

Luther's confidence did not fail him. To this direct command he offered his famous reply (in Latin): "Since then your serene majesty and your lordships seek a simple answer, I will give it in this manner, neither horned nor toothed: Unless I am convinced by the testimony of the Scripture or by clear reason (for I do not trust either in the pope or in councils alone, since it is well known that they have often erred and contradicted themselves), I am bound by the Scriptures I have quoted and my conscience is captive to the word of God. I cannot and I will not retract anything, since it is neither safe nor right to go against conscience. [He then added in German] Here I stand. I can do no other. God help me! Amen."[13]

Despite the clarity of Luther's answer, Johann von der Ecken pressed farther: "Abandon your conscience, Martin, for your conscience errs. You will never be able to prove that the councils have erred in questions of faith; at most they have erred in questions of discipline." Luther rejoined, "I can prove it." But before discussion went farther, the angered emperor gestured for Luther to be removed from the imperial court. Some thought that Luther was being arrested. Spanish soldiers shouted, "Al fuego, al fuego!" (Into the fire!) Upon exiting, Luther was greeted by throngs of jubilant citizens celebrating much as they would the victory of a tournament. Their voices rang with cheer as Luther raised his hands and exclaimed, "I made it through! I made it through!"[14]

Charles V was unimpressed with Luther (to put it mildly) and pronounced him an outlaw. About his infamous German renegade, the emperor said, "This devil in the habit of a monk ... has brought together ancient errors into one stinking puddle, and has invented new ones."[15] Although Luther's stand marked the climax of his defense before Charles V, it was by no means the end of the drama.

---

13. The phrase "here I stand, I can do no other" is absent from the official transcript of the proceedings at Worms. It may have been added to Luther's words afterward by a printer (von Loewenich, *Martin Luther*, 195).

14. Ibid.

15. Bruce L. Shelley, *Church History in Plain Language* (Waco: Word, 1982), 260.

Not even Hollywood could produce a more colorful conclusion to Luther's story. As he and two companions rolled along a wooded path, their wagon was ambushed. "Armed horsemen fell upon the party and with much cursing and show of violence dragged Luther to the ground. The one companion, privy to the ruse, played his part and roundly berated the abductors. They placed Luther upon a horse and led him for a whole day by circuitous roads through the woods until at dusk loomed up against the sky the massive contours of Wartburg Castle. At eleven o'clock in the night the party reined up before the gates."[16]

It was all a secret plot concocted by Fredrick III, elector of Luther's home, Saxony. As a supporter of Luther, Frederick decided to hide him away, giving strict orders to those involved not to divulge the details. The plan was so strategically arranged and perfectly executed that many of Luther's close friends thought that they'd heard the last of their old friend Martin. When the horses of Luther and his newfound abductor friends clattered across the drawbridge of Frederick's castle, Luther entered the ancient fortress to find smiling faces and a warm welcome.

It was critical for Luther to remain incognito. He lodged in a room with a retractable ladder. The need to stay out of sight was especially urgent until his hair and beard grew long enough to disguise his face. In exchange for his monk's habit, he dressed as a noble knight. In this environment he would remain for ten months. To everyone in the castle and around town he was known as Sir George.

Before being snatched from his wagon, Luther managed to grab his Hebrew Old Testament and Greek New Testament. Without the aid of a dictionary, he studied them carefully, and in a feat to flabbergast the most precocious Bible student, Luther translated the entire New Testament into German from the Greek text. In this act, Luther followed the footsteps of John Wycliffe, who over a century before had promoted the translation of Scripture into English (even

---

16. Bainton, *Here I Stand*, 150.

though Wycliffe operated from the Latin Vulgate and not the original languages of Hebrew and Greek). Luther's translation of the New Testament highlights the fundamental issue with which both men wrestled—the need for God's people to have God's Word. Oxford scholar Alister McGrath sheds light on this issue:

> At its heart, the emergence and growth of Protestantism concerned one of the most fundamental questions that can confront any religion: Who has the authority to define its faith? Institutions or individuals? Who has the right to interpret its foundational document, the Bible?
>
> Protestantism took its stand on the right of individuals to interpret the Bible for themselves rather than be forced to submit to "official" interpretations handed down by popes or other centralized religious authorities. For Martin Luther, perhaps the most significant of the first generation of Protestant leaders, the traditional authority of clerical institutions had led to the degradation and distortion of the Christian faith. Renewal and reformation were urgently needed. And if the medieval church would not put its own house in order, reform would have to come from its grass roots—from the laity.[17]

One need not be a Luther scholar to know that Luther had clay feet. His statements about Jews, Muslims, and most others who disagreed with him range from insensitive, to shameful, to outright injurious. Ironically, however, some of these statements, the reasonable ones at least, contribute to his appeal. They reveal that Luther was a *real* person, gastronomic discharges and all.[18] Perhaps this authenticity is part of the reason why he was so influential.

From my perspective and that of this book, Luther's greatest contribution is twofold: a return to Scripture as the supreme authority, what theologians call *sola Scriptura*, and the good news that salvation

---

17. Alister McGrath, *Christianity's Dangerous Idea* (New York: Harper One, 2007), 3.
18. Luther's chronic intestinal maladies made him famous for discussing the sort of flatulant experiences that are commonly exhibited by junior high boys.

is a gift accessed by faith alone. Both of these topics will be addressed in subsequent chapters, but before getting there, we will consider another popular reason for Catholic defection—the elevation of the desire to know God through personal relationship over the observance of rules.

EXCURSUS: SOLA SCRIPTURA

As mentioned earlier, Evangelicals insist on the supremacy of the written word, what we call *sola Scriptura* or Scripture alone, because the text is inspired by God. Second Timothy 3:16–17 says, "All Scripture is God-breathed and is useful for teaching, rebuking, correcting and training in righteousness, so that the man of God may be thoroughly equipped for every good work." The same cannot be said of the Catholic magisterium.

My purpose here is to explain what Evangelicals believe concerning Scripture alone. Because there are many fine defenses of the position already in print and on the web, I'm not inclined to rehash them here. This is the sort of debate that requires a thorough examination, not a quick listing of prooftexts. If you're interested in reading an argument on behalf of Scripture alone, I would recommend the book *Roman Catholics and Evangelicals: Agreements and Differences* by Norman L. Geisler and Ralph E. MacKenzie.

A distillation of what Evangelicals mean by "Scripture alone" is found in *The Chicago Statement on Biblical Inerrancy*, crafted by more than two hundred Evangelical leaders in October 1978. It begins with the following words: "The authority of Scripture is a key issue for the Christian church in this and every age. Those who profess faith in Jesus Christ as Lord and Savior are called to show the reality of their discipleship by humbly and faithfully obeying God's written Word. To stray from Scripture in faith or conduct is disloyalty to our Master. Recognition of the total truth and trustworthiness of Holy Scripture is essential to a full grasp and adequate confession of its authority."

While all nineteen articles of the *Chicago Statement* relate to "Scripture alone" in some way, number 2 strikes at its heart: "We affirm that the Scriptures are the supreme written norm by which God binds the conscience, and that the authority of the church is subordinate to that of Scripture. We deny that church creeds, councils, or declarations have authority greater than or equal to the authority of the Bible."

As we considered in previous chapters, Christian authority has everything to do with how the presence of Jesus extends into the world. If, as Catholics believe, the inspired revelation of Jesus is manifest in her magisterium, then you have yourself an inspired church. If, however, the inspired revelation of Jesus is in the written word alone, then Scripture is the supreme authority. On this point, the *Chicago Statement* offers another helpful summary: "By authenticating each other's authority, Christ and Scripture coalesce into a single fount of authority. The biblically interpreted Christ and the Christ-centered, Christ-proclaiming Bible are from this standpoint one. As from the face of inspiration we infer that what Scripture says, God says, so from the revealed relation between Jesus Christ and Scripture we may equally declare that what Scripture says, Christ says."

A qualification is in order. Scripture alone should not undermine one's appreciation of biblically rooted traditions. Certain standards, routines, and customs may not be explicitly stated in a book, chapter, and verse of the Bible, but they nonetheless provide forms in which to encounter and express authentic faith. These conventions will naturally look different depending on one's context. So long as they are consistent with Scripture, such traditions should be employed for the glory of God. This particular caveat is taken up more fully in chapter 7 under the heading "Beware of *Nuda Scriptura*."

Chapter 4

REASON TWO: PERSONAL RELATIONSHIP WITH JESUS

"Fanatics! That's what these Evangelical Christians are." This was a statement I heard and expressed myself many times. On Long Island most people are considered to be Catholic, Jewish, or in a religious drip-pan category labeled "other."

As a Catholic, I was ignorant of Protestantism. The only Evangelical people I encountered were of the fanatical "born again" variety. These folks resembled the character Euliss "Sonny" Dewey, played by Robert Duvall in *The Apostle*. You may recall the scene in which Sonny overcomes his psychosomatic demons by standing waist deep in water and baptizing himself as "the Apostle." Somehow, these wide-eyed country souls found their way to East Coast civilization, even to New York.

I remember talking to an Evangelical Christian shortly after Jeffrey Dahmer, the infamous serial murderer, was killed and it became known that he had converted to Christianity before his death. The Evangelical spoke confidently about Dahmer's conversion and asserted that if it was genuine, he would be forgiven simply because he had "trusted in Jesus." After hearing the word "grace" numerous times and the phrase "personal relationship with Jesus," I responded with an impassioned tirade. It went something like this:

"You know what annoys me most about Jeffrey Dahmer? It wasn't his cannibalism, though it was disgusting. Seventeen murders, eleven corpses in his apartment, dismembered bodies. Then there was his trial, his seemingly remorseless, motionless, regretless face; I wanted to jump through the television screen and slap him around. If evil has a face, this is it. But that is not what irritates me the most. You know the most outrageous part? His conversion! How is it that a monster like Dahmer can perpetrate such atrocities and then be totally forgiven?"

After venting my religious spleen, I completed my remarks with a statement I shall never forget. With more than a little pride I announced, "This religion of complete grace is an irresponsible cop-out, and it is why I will never become a born-again Christian."

THE JOURNEY BEGINS

My movement toward Evangelicalism began just after my commute to work one morning. Shortly after I reached my Manhattan office, my grandfather phoned. With a serious tone, he spoke a brief message: "It's your dad; come home." Somehow I knew not to ask questions. It turned out that Dad had suffered a severe heart attack. In the upcoming days I experienced intense fear as my father's life fluttered like a candle in the wind.

After a week of sitting beside Dad's hospital bed, I left my telephone job to manage the family business. It was a midsize printing company with a dozen employees. The waterline of anxiety rose with each day until eventually Mom's emotions crashed and I started having panic attacks. Into this dark valley appeared a new employee named Jan. I soon learned that she was a born-again Christian.

The latest test results indicated that my father was improving. However, a long road of rehabilitation still lay ahead. One day, while hanging up the phone with the doctor, I noticed a handwritten index card on my desk displaying Psalm 1:3: "The one who delights in the Law of the Lord is like a tree planted by streams of water that yields its fruit in its season, and its leaf does not wither. In all that he does, he prospers."

It was from Jan. Each day she prepared a Bible verse for me. Weeks earlier, I would have dismissed her notes as religious propaganda from a flaky employee, but now, after months of despair, I was attentive and collected the cards in my desk.

After weeks of declining Jan's invitation to visit her church, I finally showed up on a Wednesday night. I found the parking lot packed at (the Evangelical) Faith Church. Astonishment seized me while observing the constant flow of people walking through the entrance. I surveyed the crowd, expecting to see Sonny the Apostle, but in fact, I encountered another kind of Sonny, actually many of them. These guys resembled Sonny Corleone, played by James Caan in *The Godfather*.

After exchanging a kiss on the cheek (the customary greeting in Italian families) with Vinnie the Vise Grip, who wore a white carnation pinned to the lapel of his two thousand dollar olive-colored suit, I proceeded to take a seat in the rear pew. I use the word *pew*, but it was actually a line of interlocking cushioned chairs. The "worship center," as they called it, felt like a concert hall. The lights were dim, except for those focused on the platform. Probably because of my liturgically rich background in Catholicism, the environment left me feeling rather conspicuous, like a pound of Boar's Head ham sitting in full view on the counter of a Jewish synagogue. Thankfully, Jan arrived as the service started.

Occasionally, I looked through my peripheral vision at Jan. Her eyes remained closed as she sang. Oh, and did we sing! After forty minutes of music, the senior pastor finally entered the pulpit. His appearance and preaching style combined Al Pacino and the young Billy Graham. My attention was seized when he quoted John 15:5–6: "I am the vine; you are the branches. If a man remains in me and I in him, he will bear much fruit; apart from me you can do nothing. If anyone does not remain in me, he is like a branch that is thrown away and withers; such branches are picked up, thrown into the fire and burned."

The preacher continued:

> Humanity attempts to produce its own fruit. We run around exploring this and that religion, this and that philosophy, and by the end of the day, when we lay our heads down upon our pillows to sleep, our souls are still empty.
>
> The Bible says in Psalm 121, "I lift up my eyes to the hills. From where does my help come? My help comes from the LORD, who made heaven and earth." And what do we find when we look up to the Lord? He has told us with his own lips. Jesus promises in Matthew 11, "Come to me, all who labor and are heavy laden, and I will give you rest." In other words, lift your eyes above the horizon of this world to see the one who created you and who offers rest for your souls.
>
> In what are you resting? In what does your life find meaning and purpose? What will be there for you the second after you take your last breath and depart this world in death? Believe the Good News! Jesus the Messiah died for our sins, rose from the dead, reigns beside the Father, and calls humanity to embrace him as King.
>
> Everyone on earth faces the same fundamental choice. Will we continue to live independent of Christ, in restlessness of soul, eventually to be gathered like a useless branch into a pile to be burned? Or will we submit to his authority and abide in his peace? The former person dies in a never-ending state of alienation; the latter enjoys personal relationship with God from now into eternity. What will it be?

I don't know how to properly describe what came next, except that something within me changed. Similar to other converts like Augustine, Pascal, Luther, Newton, and countless others throughout history, there was a moment in which I encountered God in such a profound way that my life was permanently changed. To this day, I don't have a better way to describe it than with the words of Charles Wesley in his famous hymn "And Can It Be That I Should Gain?":

Long my imprisoned spirit lay,
fast bound in sin and nature's night;
Thine eye diffused a quickening ray,
I woke, the dungeon flamed with light;
My chains fell off, my heart was free;
I rose, went forth and followed Thee.

As the service concluded, the pastor invited visitors with questions to speak with one of the ushers designated by a white carnation. I asked Jan for a few moments of solitude, after which I looked around and spotted my friend Vinnie the Vise Grip. As I reintroduced myself, he quickly reached inside his breast pocket. His response seemed abrupt. Perhaps it was his barrel chest and infamous last name that instilled fear in me. During the brief moment when the glistening diamonds of his pinky ring vanished behind his suit coat, I shuddered to think what was coming next. Then he pulled out a slim paperback copy of John's gospel, which he handed me, assuring me that I would be in his prayers. A moment later, Jan arrived. I didn't have the words to describe my experience to her, but eventually she understood.

SANCTIONED STEAK

The next chapter of my life was perhaps the most illuminating part of the journey. Only months after Dad returned from the hospital, I took a position with the Martin J. Moran Company, a professional fundraising firm. Our office was based in Manhattan's Penn Plaza, but campaigns had me working in different parts of the country. I became the token Italian in a company full of Irishmen. We enjoyed a lot of laughs.

The educational opportunities of the fundraising position exceeded that of the telephone company. Some experiences in the Catholic Church were especially instructive. For example, I went to a black-tie affair held at the Breakers Resort on Palm Beach Island. In a gigantic dinner room sat a packed audience of wealthy potential donors. Before the bishop opened in prayer, our team reviewed the agenda one last time. It was then we discovered the blunder. All of the campaign elements were in place—volunteers, video, brochures—the problem was the food. On the menu was an entree of filet mignon, twice-baked potato, and a vegetable. At any other time of the year, steak would have been great; unfortunately, this particular Friday was during Lent, a special religious season when Catholics abstain from eating meat. To consume meat on a Friday during Lent constitutes a sin. If one should die after doing so, it would put them into the flames of purgatory (or perhaps worse). This was a serious problem!

In actuality, many Catholics eat meat on Friday during Lent, but they don't usually do it when dining with the bishop and clergy. Further, it is unthinkable that the Catholic Church would host such a meal. The salad and a dinner roll would buy us about twenty minutes. The Lord's multiplying of fish crossed my mind more than once.

While our team of fundraisers nervously stared at one another in silent bewilderment, the bishop spoke. He reiterated what we already knew about Lenten food laws and the implications for our predicament. He continued, "As the bishop, I have the authority to declare a special dispensation which will allow us to eat meat during Lent. If there is ever a time for such a provision, it is now." I then watched the bishop pray and announce the menu, and before guests connected the doctrinal dots, he pronounced a special blessing to sanction the meal. My eyes turned toward old Joe Sedlak, who sat beside me thinking that if he had choked on his steak and died apart from the bishop's blessing, he would have been roasted. But now, after the bishop's prayer, he could feast in peace.

From an Evangelical point of view, clerical authority of this kind stretches incredulity to the breaking point. Because salvation is understood to be by grace alone, our jaws drop and we look with wonder at our Catholic friends. Even so, the bishop's announcement makes sense in the context of Catholic theology. If authority is vested in the bishops to the extent that they mediate forgiveness and sanctifying grace, then such priestly action follows logically.

That evening, I left the Breakers finally understanding that the issue of church authority is the fulcrum which separates Catholics from Evangelicals. Do you recognize authority to be found in the bishops by means of apostolic succession? If you say yes, you are a Catholic. If instead you see ultimate authority to be in Scripture alone, you are an Evangelical.

RELATIONSHIP OVER RULES

Hand in hand with the belief that Scripture alone forms the supreme authority for Christian faith is the conviction that our knowledge of the Lord is personal and direct in nature. Like a father relating to his beloved child, God holds the church in his heart. Such personalized affection is central to the Father's approach.

It's important to note that some Catholics have excelled in cultivating this form of devotion. Church history speaks of numerous mystics and saints, such as Thomas Merton and Dorothy Day, who grappled intensely with the personal dimensions of God.[1] Yet among many Catholics today, particularly the former Catholics whom we interviewed, the personal facet of faith was missing.

When we questioned ex-Catholics about the way they previously related to God, they often described their experience in terms of an "array of rules" which was imposed upon them. Whether it is the doctrine of limbo (which was recently nixed by the Catholic Church), eating meat on Fridays during Lent, or the necessity of confessing one's sins to a priest, the assertions of Rome as to who is in mortal sin and who is in a state of grace were less than persuasive.

If I had a dime for every priest-in-the-confessional-box story I heard in our focus groups, I would have at least enough money for a venti cappuccino at Starbucks. For instance, at age twelve Susan goes

1. The legacy of Catholic spirituality is long and rich. Faithful individuals like Augustine, Francis of Assisi, Blaise Pascal, Brother Lawrence, Gregory of Nyssa, Hans Urs von Balthasar, Ignatius Loyola, John of the Cross, Teresa of Avila, Therese of Lisieux, and more recent figures like Evelyn Underhill have inspired many of God's people to pursue Christ with greater zeal.

to help her invalid grandfather on his farm during the summer. After several months she returns home and within days she visits her parish for confession. In the confessional box she tells the priest that it had been four months since her last confession on account of her visit with Grandpa. In response, the priest launches into a tirade about dishonest girls who neglect the sacrament of penance in order to play outside in the warm months. Susan never again confessed her sins to a priest.

By relaying this account, I don't mean to besmirch priests in the confessional. Most of the priests I know are caring and compassionate pastors who relish their role as spiritual shepherds. No doubt, the priest whom Susan visited was having a bad day. However, when this kind of story is repeated again and again, a composite picture starts to emerge. For many ex-Catholics, the disillusionment caused by this picture is just as vivid today as it was the day when they departed from their Catholic parish.

Unlike the rules-oriented experience of many Catholics, the Bible describes salvation in terms that are most intimate and inviting. As Jesus put it, "Greater love has no one than this: that he lay down his life for his friends. You are my friends if you do what I command. I no longer call you servants, because a servant does not know his master's business. Instead, I have called you friends, for everything that I learned from my Father I have made known to you" (John 15:13–15).

When I was ordained at College Church, someone gave me a hand-drawn picture of Jesus carrying a lamb upon his shoulders, which is now framed and displayed in our home. This image of the small, weak creature nestled closely to the Lord's neck comes to mind when I consider the quality of this relationship. Jesus, the friend of tax collectors and sinners, is a whole lot more, but nothing less, than our friend.

Maybe by now you are beginning to wonder how Catholics and Evangelicals can reach such different conclusions when we share a common New Testament. The next chapter sheds light on why it is so.

Chapter 5

REASON THREE: DIRECT ACCESS TO GOD

Few things embody Italian exuberance more than life in a piazza after a World Cup victory. The collective elation borders on rioting (with police in body armor actually standing in the wings). All appearances of being a civilized nation are abandoned as flags, fireworks, and flares are elevated above swarming crowds. A volcanic eruption of Mount Vesuvius is mild by comparison.

In the summer of 2006, I enjoyed one such celebration when the Italian soccer team defeated Germany in double overtime during the closing moments of the semifinal World Cup game. After the blazing soccer ball reached the back of the German net, apartments throughout Italy exploded with cheers. The final goal was replayed several times along with Pavarotti's version of "Nessun dorma" from Puccini's *Turandot.* With his three climactic *vinceros* at the end of the aria (translated "I shall win"), the ball rose, arched, and landed sweetly and safely in the corner of the net. The subsequent unleashing of euphoria defied description. Waving, cheering, and chanting resounded throughout the streets and into the cobblestone piazzas. The central fountain of the Piazza Campo dei Fiori (Field of Flowers) became a stage on which the most clamorous stood and chanted, "C'í non salta un Tedesco è!" (He who does not jump is a German!) Soon everyone in the piazza was laughing, jumping, and singing.

As the evening festivity continued, the terraces around the piazza filled with spectators. From one such window emerged an elderly gentleman in his undershirt, enjoying a smoke. A few young men noticed the resemblance of this fellow to the late Fascist dictator Benito Mussolini. They shouted, "Look up, look up!" and began calling to the second-story window, "Il Duce, Il Duce!" (Mussolini's nickname, translated "the Leader.") Soon others were allured by this phenomenon. The old man played the part with delight. Initially, I thought he was a professional actor, since he performed so well; then I realized he was simply Italian. Others quickly joined in, and soon the entire piazza was looking to the same window where the old man with the prominent hooked nose and protruding chin enjoyed his moment of fame. The crowd continued to chant, "Duce, Duce, Duce!" as the Benito look-alike waved and blew kisses to his adoring fans.

Among the various lessons I learned in the Roman piazza is the importance of having a leader. God has created us to follow him; men and women cannot function otherwise. However, from the Greek philosopher Protagoras to the blue-eyed Sinatra of Hoboken, man has measured meaning by himself and has sought to live his own way.

Catholics and Evangelicals agree that men and women are designed to depend on God and not live as delusional demigods who create their own destiny. Scripture describes us as sheep whom God leads into green pastures. When a sheep wanders off by himself, it isn't long before danger befalls him. To avoid this calamity, the shepherd extends nurture and protection. Such loving care is graphically expressed by Charles Spurgeon in the following story.

> One evening, in 1861, as General Garibaldi was going home, he met a Sardinian shepherd lamenting the loss of a lamb out of his flock. Garibaldi at once turned to his staff and announced his intention of scouring the mountain in search of the lamb. A grand expedition was organized. Lanterns were

> brought, and old officers of many a campaign started off, full of zeal, to hunt the fugitive. But no lamb was found, and the soldiers were ordered to their beds. The next morning Garibaldi's attendant found him in bed, fast asleep. He was surprised at this, for the General was always up before anybody else. The attendant went off softly and returned in half-an-hour. Garibaldi still slept. After another delay, the attendant awoke him. The General rubbed his eyes, and so did his attendant when he saw the old warrior take from under the covering the lost lamb and bid him convey it to the shepherd. The General had kept up the search through the night until he had found it. Even so does the Good Shepherd go in search of His lost sheep until He finds them.[1]

"We all like sheep have gone astray; we have turned—every one—to his own way," says the prophet Isaiah (53:6 ESV). In John's gospel Jesus says, "I am the good shepherd; I know my sheep and my sheep know me—just as the Father knows me and I know the Father—and I lay down my life for the sheep" (John 10:14–15). In response to these statements, all Christians say, "Amen." Jesus, the Lamb of God who takes away the sin of the world, died, rose, and is now seated beside the Father in heaven. Up to this point Catholics and Evangelicals are of one mind. However, disagreement comes with the question that usually follows: who represents the Good Shepherd on earth?

THE PAPA

In the city of Rome there is another window before which onlookers cry, "Look up, look up!" But this frame is filled with a pious man. He is located just 3.6 kilometers from Campo di Fiore at the Vatican. From his studio window overlooking St. Peter's Square, the pope stands to celebrate the Angelus noon prayer and greet faithful pilgrims

1. Charles Spurgeon, *The Best of C. H. Spurgeon* (Grand Rapids, MI: Baker, 1978), 117.

who gather to see him and receive his blessing. These faithful Catholics who gather in the Petrine Piazza look up and in unison they call out, "Papa, Papa," meaning "Father."

When most people think of Roman Catholicism, the pope may very well be the first thing that comes to mind. The pope is the only person who is prayed for at every Catholic Mass. Among the irreligious, it is common to hear someone affirm a proposition with the rhetorical question, "Is the pope Catholic?" Whether it is a Protestant in Colorado Springs, an Orthodox Jew in Far Rockaway, Brooklyn, or a Muslim in Pakistan, virtually everyone recognizes the pope to be the earthly leader of Roman Catholicism. Yet most people probably don't know much more about him than that he lives in Rome and works in a church. In the interest of acquiring a deeper understanding, let's hear the Catholic Church speak for itself. The *Catechism of the Catholic Church* offers the following comments:

> To proclaim the faith and to plant his reign, Christ sends his apostles and their successors. He gives them a share in his own mission. From this they receive the power to act in his person.[2]

> The Lord made St. Peter the visible foundation of his Church. He entrusted the keys of the Church to him. The bishop of the Church of Rome, successor to St. Peter, is "head of the college of bishops, the Vicar of Christ and Pastor of the universal Church on earth."[3]

There are numerous excerpts from the *Catechism* one might choose to describe the papal office. I selected these paragraphs because they convey the pope's nature and function in the church. Simply put, Jesus made Peter the visible head of his church when he gave him the "keys" to the kingdom. This authority, which the keys symbolize, is exercised in three ways:

2. *Catechism of the Catholic Church*, para. 934.
3. Ibid., para. 935.

1. *Teaching*: the pope is authorized to teach and interpret divine revelation with authority.
2. *Sanctifying*: in addition to overseeing the administration of the sacraments, the pope has authority to ordain priests or other bishops.
3. *Ruling*: the pope rules the "universal church on earth."

The pope's authority is graphically depicted. For instance, look at the papal insignia below for the three ways in which it is symbolized.

The crossed keys depict the authority of the kingdom which Jesus gave to Simon Peter in Matthew 16. The key to the left (usually depicted as silver) signifies the power to bind and loose on earth, and the one on the right (depicted as gold) the power to bind and loose in heaven.[4] The second symbol is the so-called tiara, or triple crown, located between the keys. It represents the three functions described above: teaching, sanctifying, and ruling. Third, the gold

4. Another interpretation says that the silver key represents binding and the golden key represents loosing.

cross mounted on top of the tiara conveys the sovereignty of Jesus which the pope exercises.[5]

As the last couple of quotes state, Christ's authority is passed on to Peter and to subsequent popes by means of "succession." Accordingly, after a pope has died, cardinals gather in a conclave at the Sistine Chapel to appoint a successor through rounds of voting. This practice is akin to what we observe in the first chapter of Acts, where the Holy Spirit directed the apostles to choose Matthias as the replacement of Judas. Perhaps the following illustration will help to clarify how papal succession works.

Among the largest organisms on earth is the mighty aspen tree. It is commonly found on America's northwest coast. Supposedly, there is one aspen in the state of Utah weighing over six thousand tons. For those who don't have a calculator handy, that's twelve million pounds.

One can't help but wonder how the aspen can grow to the heavens and yet live for only one hundred years. In view of its enormous size, such a life span is relatively brief. The reason for such brevity is the tree's origin. Instead of starting with a seed, the aspen begins with a simple limb. This limb grows down into the soil and eventually takes on a life of its own. The process of sending out limbs continues from one tree to another until a single aspen spawns thousands of other trees. Looking at the forest, the various trees appear to stand independently of one another, but in fact all of them are organically derived from the initial one. The original limb decays in obscurity among its children, who continue to pass on life for thousands of years.

---

5. Perhaps the most succinct explanation of the pope's role is found in the *Catholic Encyclopedia*: "The Bishop of Rome ... exercises universal jurisdiction over the whole Church as the Vicar of Christ and the Successor of St. Peter. The term 'pope' derives from the Latin for 'father' ... In Western Christianity, this term refers to the Roman Pontiff, called His Holiness the Pope, who governs the universal Church as the successor to St. Peter ... who possesses, 'by virtue of his office ... supreme, full, immediate, and universal ordinary jurisdiction power in the Church'" (Canon 331, quoted in Peter M. Stravinskas, *Catholic Encyclopedia* [Huntingdon, IN: Our Sunday Visitor, 1991], 761).

The life cycle of the aspen illustrates how immediate, tangible objects (like trees or popes) share life with what precedes them. Although the original aspen has died, it lives on through successive generations. Likewise, Catholics assert, from the death of Peter to Benedict XVI, the papal office continues.[6]

SPEAKING FOR GOD

Contrary to popular belief, the pope doesn't rule the Catholic Church alone. Leadership also involves the "college of bishops."[7] This significant development of Vatican II is often overlooked by Evangelicals. Catholic bishops share in the pope's authority (in terms of teaching, sanctifying, and ruling) as a unified council, with the Roman pontiff as their "head."[8]

Operating from texts like Luke 10:16, in which Jesus says to the seventy-two disciples, "He who hears you, hears me," the pope and the bishops purport to speak on behalf of God, providing the church with the authorized interpretation of Scripture and tradition. Together the pope and bishops comprise what Catholics call the "magisterium."[9] The magisterium is defined by the *Catechism* as "the living teaching office of the Church, whose task it is to give as authentic interpretation of the word of God, whether in its written form (Sacred Scripture), or in the form of Tradition. The magisterium ensures the Church's fidelity to the teaching of the Apostles in matters of faith and morals."[10]

You'll notice in the *Catechism*'s definition that the teaching office is described as "living." Don't miss this detail. The magisterium is understood to be living, just as the person of Christ is living in and

6. According to Catholic teaching, the papal office succeeds not from the previous pope but from Peter himself. Thus, each pope is thought to be the successor of Peter. Lon Allison inspired the aspen tree analogy.
7. *Catechism of the Catholic Church*, para. 935, 938.
8. Ibid., para. 883.
9. A helpful primer on the Catholic magisterium has been written by the late Avery Cardinal Dulles, SJ: *Magisterium: Teacher and Guardian of the Faith* (Naples: Sapientia, 2007).
10. *Catechism of the Catholic Church*, para. 85, 890, 2033. Avery Cardinal Dulles, "The Freedom of Theology," *First Things* 183 (May 2008): 20.

through his church. Since the church is the living body of Christ on earth,[11] Christ is thought to speak through it, particularly through the church's head, the pope. In terms of our aspen tree analogy, we notice how the one original tree continues to develop beyond its death. Likewise, the magisterium is regarded as a "living" office which brings to light truth from God's Word for each new generation.

Out of the magisterium comes the Catholic teaching of infallibility—the idea that the church can definitively proclaim a particular doctrine to be without error when it is done by the pope in union with the bishops.[12] Hopefully, one can understand a little bit more why such a teaching arose. If indeed the infallible Jesus were to speak through the magisterium, it is logical to think that such revelation would be (or could be) infallible.[13]

DISAGREEMENT OVER THE PAPACY

During summers when I was home from Bible college, I worked as a chauffeur. The position was ideal for two reasons. The customers whom I drove from Manhattan to the Hamptons tended to be interesting conversation partners, and the long hours of waiting outside opera halls and stadiums provided time to study Greek grammar. It was a dream job.

There was one client I shall never forget even though I can't remember his name. Somehow we got on the topic of religion when he expressed his frustration with "those irritating born-again Christians." Since he obviously assumed that I was a fellow Catholic (probably on

---

11. For more on this, see the encyclical by Pope Pius XII titled *Mystici Corporis* [On the Mystical Body of Christ], 29 June 1943.

12. For a helpful explanation of the official criteria for papal infallibility, see Avery Cardinal Dulles, "Infallibility: The Terminology," in *Teaching Authority and Infallibility in the Church*, ed. Paul C. Empie, et al. (Minneapolis: Augsburg, 1978), 79–80.

13. We commonly misunderstand the dogma of infallibility. Only when the pope speaks *ex cathedra* (from the chair) are his words regarded as though Christ were directly speaking (also described in terms of *de fide*, "that which must be believed"). Since 1870, the only strictly infallible declaration of the pope has been of Mary's assumption into heaven, which Pius XII pronounced in 1950.

account of my Italian last name), I decided to keep my cards close to my chest until he was finished venting.

His biggest beef concerned the "chummy chummy" way that Evangelicals approach God. If I may paraphrase, his tirade went something like this: "Protestants think that they possess authority like the pope. Take, for instance, my cousin; he belongs to a born-again church which always talks about a 'personal relationship' with Christ. He refers to Jesus as his 'friend' and calls the Lord by his first name ('Jesus,' as opposed to his last name, 'Christ'). I want to sit my cousin down to watch *On the Waterfront* so he can see what a holy person really looks like. Priests are the only ones who deserve to call God 'friend.' "

I resisted the temptation to point out that Christ is not Jesus' last name but rather his messianic title, but I couldn't ignore his dogmatic moratorium against the language of "friend." As innocently as possible, I asked, "How do you explain the fact that Jesus uses the term 'friend' three separate times in John 15 to describe his followers? Or how do you explain God calling Abraham his 'friend' simply because Abe believed in God's promise?"

My Catholic passenger paused and then asked, "Did you say you were a Catholic?"

Later in the book I'll discuss the Evangelical tendency of being "chummy chummy" with Almighty God, but for now, I want to continue to explore the Evangelical concern about the papacy and priesthood with help from one of my favorite Roman Catholic authors.

Dr. Eamon Duffy is Professor of the History of Christianity at Cambridge. His thirty-five years of research has included a detailed examination of the papacy. His most popular treatment of the topic is his book *Saints and Sinners: A History of the Popes*.[14] I like Duffy's writing for several reasons: as a devout Catholic he is concerned with what faith looks like on the ground. His writing style is especially lucid and

14. Eamon Duffy, *Saints and Sinners: A History of the Popes* (New Haven, CT: Yale Univ. Press, 2002).

engaging, and he has a firm grasp on both theology and history. For our purposes here, his explanation of the papacy illuminates many of the concerns of former Catholics.

In our discussions with ex-Catholics about the papacy, two issues rose to the top. First is the Catholic assertion that Christianity must have a visible authority structure rooted in the pope and bishops. The purpose of this structure is explained in Ludwig Ott's *Fundamentals of Catholic Dogma*: "Without an authoritative teaching office there is no certain norm for the purity of doctrine or for the administration of the Sacraments."[15] So the argument goes, without the papacy, there is no head; without the head, there is no body; without the body, there is no church. Therefore, Evangelicals who fail to submit to the pope's authority are in effect failing to submit to Christ.[16]

But should all Christians—Catholics, Eastern Orthodox, and Protestants—submit to the pope as Christ's God-ordained representative on earth? Professor Duffy helps us to think through this question:

> Catholics tend to assume that the development of the papacy has been a steadfast evolution from Christ's appointment of Peter as the one who would "feed my lambs" to John Paul II's world tours and solemn pronouncements on the objectivity of morals or the non-ordainability of women. Most people are vaguely aware that papal authority as we know it was not exercised by the early popes, but the later powers of the popes are assumed by Catholics to have been implicit in the more limited authority the early popes did actually possess. History, alas, is not so simple: the development of the papacy is not in any straightforward sense a matter of the steady unfolding of implicit powers and functions. Authority is never a matter

15. Ludwig Ott, *Fundamentals of Catholic Dogma* (Rockford, IL: Tan Books and Publishers, 1974), 301.

16. Sebastian Tromp, SJ, *Corpus Christi quod est ecclesia*, trans. Ann Condit (New York: Vantage, 1960), 194–95.

> of paper theory or mere status: it is embodied in real powers, and takes its meaning from the exercise of those powers. Yet many of the most characteristic functions of the papacy, like the appointment of bishops, are very recent indeed, and originated less in any scriptural or patristic basis than in the vagaries of history and in the confusion of roles which were in theory quite distinct.[17]

> Neither Paul, Acts nor any of the Gospels tells us anything direct about Peter's death, and none of them even hints that the special role of Peter could be passed on to any single "successor." There is, therefore, nothing directly approaching a papal theory in the pages of the New Testament.[18]

The second concern of ex-Catholics toward the papacy involves the pope's clerical function, his relationship to the priesthood. Since Evangelicals disagree with the sacramental hierarchy of the church on biblical grounds, we don't see any need to approach God through the mediation of a priest (the hierarchy which connects pope to cardinals to archbishops to bishops, monsignors, priests, archdeacons, and deacons). Evangelicals regard all believers to be priests who enjoy direct access to God by virtue of being in Christ, who is our great High Priest. Ordained pastors are still important to pass on the faith (2 Tim. 2:2), but not as priestly mediators who extend or deny access to God with sacramental authority. Once again, Duffy helps by explaining how this mediating role of ordained priests is fundamental to Catholic religion:

> Priesthood was forever, and to be a priest was to be ordained into a state of life as ancient and unearthly as the Church itself. No priests, no sacraments; and no sacraments, no

17. Eamon Duffy, *Faith of Our Fathers: Reflections on Catholic Tradition* (London: Continuum, 2004), 68.
18. Duffy, *Saints and Sinners*, 2, 6.

> Church. Christ had invented—or, in view of Melchizedek, maybe reinvented—priests at the Last Supper, ordaining the apostles to say Mass and hear confessions, and that was what priests had gone on doing ever since. The priests who lived in the local parochial house might wear black serge suits, play hurling, and sport bicycle-clips, but in every other respect they were just what the apostles had been, and did just what the apostles did. The clergy, and the work of the clergy, were part of the apostolic timelessness of the Church. They were holy, a race apart, their special status symbolized by and derived from their celibacy.[19]

I have a feeling my Catholic friend in the limo would have liked this paragraph, for it communicates the same conviction that he expressed. It is a mindset that elevates priests to a higher spiritual plane above laypeople. Evangelicals, on the other hand, see this kind of distinction as a basic flaw of Catholicism, especially as it concerns celibacy. Every person I interviewed, bar none, considered celibacy to be a problem that moves beyond the priesthood to affect the entire Catholic community. The reason is because of the perceived relationship between celibacy and priests perpetrating pedophilia. Numerous books have been written on the topic by Catholic authors. The most recent one I've read is *The Coming Catholic Church* by David Gibson. Rather than my addressing the issue as an Evangelical, it seems more appropriate to direct readers to an honest internal critique like Gibson's. The one point I want to make is that from the perspective of ex-Catholics, the priesthood's immorality problem transcends the individual perpetrators and bishops who sought to exonerate them. The behavior of these men also undermines confidence in the general notion of a spiritually elevated clergy, or in Duffy's words, the "holy, race apart, special status" of the priesthood.

Some of my greatest mentors have been Catholic priests. I genuinely rise up in gratitude for their pastoral sensitivity and certainly

19. Duffy, *Faith of Our Fathers*, 98.

don't want to cast aspersions on them, or on the pope for that matter.[20] Rather, I'm interested in the question of how to access God's presence. Based on Scripture, Evangelicals contend that "there is one God and one mediator between God and men, the man Christ Jesus" (1 Tim. 2:5). Because our identity is founded in the risen Christ, we are given the privilege to "approach the throne of grace with confidence" (Heb. 4:16). This is possible for one reason, because the Lord "appeared once for all at the end of the ages to do away with sin by the sacrifice of himself" (9:26). Therefore, as God's children, we "fix our eyes on Jesus, the author and perfecter of our faith" (12:2).

In the next chapter we'll consider two individuals from the Reformation period who had conversion experiences not unlike Luther's, but who ultimately chose to side with the papacy over their own consciences. Their names are Ignatius of Loyola and Cardinal Gasparo Contarini. Among other lessons, these men exemplify the essential commitment of devout Catholics.

20. Pope Benedict XVI, it should be noted, deserves credit for emphasizing the personal dimensions of faith in exceptional ways. For instance, in describing life in the Holy Spirit, he writes, "This is essential: the Christian ethic is not born from a system of commandments but is a consequence of our friendship with Christ" (*Saint Paul* [San Francisco: Ignatius, 2009], 88). Such an emphasis, it seems, is more commonly expressed today than in previous generations.

Chapter 6

A PORTRAIT OF CATHOLIC FAITH: LOYOLA AND CONTARINI

In 1521, the same year as Luther's "stand" at the Diet of Worms, another Catholic engaged in battle. Unlike Luther, however, this man was on the emperor's side. As the French armies descended upon the north of his country, this Spanish nobleman had the unfortunate experience of stepping in front of a flying cannonball. The impact shattered his leg. During his convalescence he pored over the only two books available to him in the hospital: a fourteenth-century *Life of Christ* and a thirteenth-century Dominican work on the saints titled *Golden Legend*. Because it was determined that his leg was improperly set, it was broken and reset, and he was forced to remain in bed. However, his heart embarked upon a spiritual journey that changed the course of history.

Ignatius of Loyola (1491 – 1556) was the man. At the Benedictine Abbey of Montserrat, he forsook his ambition for advancement in the Castilian court by hanging up his armor and adopting the garb of a beggar. In dependence upon God alone, he gave himself to such austerities as fasting for days, wrapping his flesh in a barbed girdle, and publicly begging for alms. As one might expect, this lifestyle introduced a certain amount of depression, so much so that Ignatius considered suicide. Eventually, however, the darkness gave way to a mystical illumination which transformed his life. In his own words, he was "a new man."[1]

As Ignatius pondered his mystical experience, his religious calling took shape. In 1523 he traveled to the Holy Land. On the same road where Spanish soldiers had marched in crusade against Muslims in Jerusalem, Ignatius now walked (or limped) as a soldier for Christ. He too would lead a crusade, the nature of which eventually united men in fervent submission to Christ and the pope.

After returning to Europe, Ignatius prepared for the priesthood. He studied theology for eleven years—four in Barcelona, followed by seven at the University of Paris. While studying, Ignatius carefully recorded his ideas concerning prayer, self-examination, and submission to divine authority. These entries formed the basis of his classic work *Spiritual Exercises*. Other men eventually joined him, and in 1543 he and these six companions formed the nucleus of a movement called the Society of Jesus, or Jesuits.

CATHOLIC RENEWAL

The early Reformation was not limited to the line of Wycliffe, Huss, and Luther,[2] for distinctively *Catholic* renewal movements also were growing in size and influence. Such groups went by a variety of names, such as the Oratory of Divine Love, Barnabites, Theatines, Capuchins, and Ignatius's Jesuits. Historians often describe these groups in terms of the Catholic Reformation. The common thread between them and Protestant counterparts was a desire for a deep and genuine experience of God, one which would transform souls and nations.

Of the various reforming voices, Ignatius of Loyola's is a prime example of one that remained devoted to the Roman Catholic Church.

1. John W. O'Malley, *The First Jesuits* (Cambridge, MA: Harvard Univ. Press, 1993), 24.
2. The sixteenth century witnessed many renewal movements throughout Europe, such as the Lollards, who were concentrated in England, the Waldensians in France, the Hussites in Bohemia (Czech Republic), and *Spirituali* in Italy (Diarmaid MacCulloch, *The Reformation* [New York: Viking Penguin, 2003], 35–37).

He and his Jesuit colleagues were ardent defenders of the Catholic institution, particularly the papacy. The seriousness of this commitment is expressed in the papal edict *Regimini militantis ecclesiae* (On the Government of the Church).

The Jesuits approached spiritual renewal in such a way that their activity differed from most other religious orders. Unlike the common friar or hermit, they avoided monastic enclosures, clerical garb, and the daily routine of communal labor and worship. Similar to Protestant Reformers, they endeavored to promote dynamic faith among laypeople and enrich the structures of public life. As decades passed, they pursued this objective by establishing centers of formal education. The presence of Jesuit schools today bears witness to the scope of their vision.

Although in later years Jesuits would come to be known as aggressive adversaries of Protestantism, this was not so in the beginning. "So [for instance] when the Genevan Pierre Favre, one of Ignatius's closest associates from his Paris student days, instructed fellow Jesuits in how they should treat Lutherans, he stressed that it should be a matter of simple Christian witness, 'speaking with them familiarly on those topics which we have in common and avoiding all contentious arguments in which one party might seem to beat the other.'"[3] This amiable posture underscores the common spiritual concern shared by Catholic and Protestant leaders of renewal.

Ignatius was not the only Catholic leader who desired deeper spirituality and pursued cultural engagement. Other examples include Gasparo Contarini, Reginald Pole, Bernardino Ochino, Juan de Valdes, and Peter Vermigli. These men were part of a movement called the *Spirituali* (also called "Evangelism").[4] It was a product of Italian soil, unlike Protestantism, which developed north of the Alps.[5] In essence, it was composed of spiritually minded Catholics who believed

3. Ibid., 218.

4. Alister McGrath, *Christianity's Dangerous Idea* (New York: Harper One, 2007), 26–27.

5. Alister E. McGrath, *Iustitia Dei: A History of the Christian Doctrine of Justification*, 2nd ed. (Cambridge: Cambridge Univ. Press, 1998), 248.

that salvation ultimately hinges on God's provision of redemptive grace, accessed through faith alone, as opposed to one's pious deeds.[6]

Cardinal Gasparo Contarini, one of the *Spirituali*'s outstanding leaders, led a life that intersected with the teaching of Luther and Ignatius at critical points. Born in 1483, Contarini was the eldest of seven sons and four daughters of Alvise Contarini of Venice.[7] In Contarini's day, Italy was rife with struggles among the papacy, the Holy Roman Empire, and various regional powers. These struggles plagued the peninsula with invasions, including the sack of Rome in 1527. Spiritual and political reform were long overdue. Machiavelli's invocation of a pragmatic prince and Savonarola's bonfire of the vanities were just two examples of how Italians responded to the problem. This gloomy context provided the kindling with which the *Spirituali* ignited a flame.

Trained in philosophy at the University of Padua, Contarini was an intellectual who loved to dialog about complex issues of politics and faith, especially through letter writing. On one occasion, his close friend Tomasso Giustiniani wrote to Contarini expressing distress that even after entering the Camaldoese Order of Hermits, he failed to have any hope of salvation.[8] This greatly troubled Contarini and made him seriously ponder his own faith. Like Luther's, Contarini's angst revolved around the question of how one obtains divine forgiveness.[9]

We're not sure how long Contarini wrestled with his dark cloud of doubt, but we know that a ray of hope eventually pierced his heart. It was "on Holy Saturday of 1511" when Contarini "experienced a moment of illumination" that was likened to Luther's epiphany, after which "he was fully convinced that salvation could not be won by

6. Philip McNair, *Peter Martyr in Italy: An Anatomy of Apostasy* (Oxford: Clarendon, 1967), 1–50, quoted in Elizabeth Gleason, "On the Nature of Sixteenth-Century Italian Evangelism: Scholarship, 1953–1978," *Sixteenth Century Journal* 9, no. 3 (Autumn 1978): 7.

7. Elizabeth Gleason, *Gasparo Contarini: Venice, Rome, and Reform* (Los Angeles: Univ. of California Press, 1993), 3.

8. Felix Gilbert, *History: Choice and Commitment* (Cambridge, MA: Harvard Univ. Press, 1977), 252.

9. Dermot Fenlon, *Heresy and Obedience in Tridentine Italy: Cardinal Pole and the Counter Reformation* (Cambridge: Cambridge Univ. Press, 1972), 7.

any human act but was God's free gift; and, as in Luther's case, this conviction was accompanied by a perception that the monastery could not, for himself, procure an eternal blessedness."[10] " 'Like Luther, Contarini found in the contemplation of Christ's sacrifice the solvent of his fears, and the resolution of his anxious striving for perfection.' He understood his own works to be powerless in providing the salvation that only Christ secures."[11] This fresh discovery of Jesus' passion left Contarini awestruck. Not only did it forge an affinity with Luther's doctrine of faith alone, it also motivated Contarini to proclaim the sufficiency of the cross among Catholics.[12]

Similar to early Jesuit missionaries, Contarini believed that Roman Catholics should exemplify Christlike love toward Protestants. In his own words:

> We do not need councils, disputations, syllogisms, and excerpts from Holy Scripture to quiet the agitation of the Lutherans, but good will, love of God and neighbor, and humility of soul, as we put aside avarice and pride in our possessions and splendid domestic establishments, and convert our households to what the Gospel prescribes. This is necessary to extinguish the errors and tumults of the Lutherans. Let us not bring against them heaps of books, Ciceronion orations, subtle arguments; but uprightness of life and a humble mind cleansed of pride, only desiring Christ and the good of our neighbor. With these weapons, believe me, no dealing with the Lutherans, nay even with the Turks and Jews, could turn out badly. In this consists the duty of Christian prelates,

---

10. William J. Bouwsma, *Venice and the Defense of Republican Liberty* (Los Angeles: Univ. of California Press, 1984), 124.
11. Fenlon, *Heresy and Obedience*, 9.
12. "[Contarini] reiterated that he would live secure and without fear of his own wickedness because of Christ's mercy" (Stephen D. Bowd, *Reform before the Reformation: Vincenzo Querini and the Religious Renaissance in Italy* [Leiden: Brill, 2002], 93). Also see James B. Ross, "The Emergence of Gasparo Contarini: A Bibliographic Essay," *Church History* 41, no. 1 (March 1972), 24.

> and for this they should employ all their efforts. If they fail to do it, and rely instead on the favor of princes, arguments, authorities, and masses of books, they will, in my opinion, accomplish little. This is my firm conviction.[13]

COLLOQUY OF REGENSBURG

Whenever we identify individuals as representative figures of this or that ideology, we are in danger of oversimplification. This sort of jamming a square peg into a round hole inevitably damages the square peg, and depending on how hard we shove, perhaps also the hole. No person fits perfectly into a profile. Nevertheless, profiles serve a valuable purpose in showing what a particular belief system looks like on the ground in relationship to others. Therefore, with caution we will proceed to explore how Luther, Ignatius, and Contarini serve as representative figures.

In April 1541 Charles V, emperor of the Holy Roman Empire, organized an imperial conclave to unify his empire against threats from the outside.[14] Simultaneously, he engineered a theological conference at Regensburg to accompany the diplomatic sessions. Because of the close connection between church and state, achieving religious unity between the opposing forces of the Roman Catholic Church and Protestants was an important step toward his goal of establishing political coherency.[15]

By the 1540s, the Protestant churches had solidified their theological positions. In 1530 the Augsburg Confession had been established; John Calvin completed his first edition of his magnum opus, *Institutes*

---

13. *Confutatio articulorum seu quaestionum Lutheranorum*, in Gasparo Contarini, *Gegenreformatorische schriften (1530c.–1542)*, ed. Friedrich Hunermann, in William J. Bouwsma, *Venice and the Defense of Republican Liberty: Renaissance Values in the Age of the Counter Reformation* (Berkeley: Univ. of California Press, 1968), 126.

14. The primary enemies of Charles V were the Turks and the French (J. van der Walt, "John Calvin as a Person," in *Our Reformational Tradition: A Rich Vocation and Lasting Vocation*, ed. Institute for Reformational Studies, 155–75 [Silverton: Promedia Publications, 1984], 159).

15. Heinz Mackensen, "Contarini's Theological Role at Ratisbon in 1541," *Archive for Reformationsgeschichte* 51 (1960): 36.

of the Christian Religion, in 1536. Moreover, doctrinal positions like Luther's justification by faith alone had become familiar throughout Europe. All of this meant that what Charles V was calling for, in the unification of Catholics and Protestants, was no small feat.[16]

You might say that the meeting at Regensburg was a last-ditch effort to reconcile Catholic and Protestant factions. After unsuccessful attempts at ecumenical accord at Hagenau (1540) and Worms (1541), most people had lost hope for reunification. It was in the twelfth hour that Cardinal Gasparo Contarini was sent by the pope to meet the emperor to encourage positive dialog. An agenda was prepared and representatives from each side were chosen.[17]

In a matching of religious "dream teams," bright sparks from both sides were chosen to participate. On April 21, 1541, the emperor announced their names. Philip Melanchthon, Martin Bucer, and Johann Pistorius represented the Protestants (the young John Calvin was present on the sideline). For the Roman Catholic Church were Johann Eck, Johann Gropper, and Julius Pflug. Cardinal Gasparo Contarini presided, representing Pope Paul III.[18] The theological meeting came to be called the Colloquy of Regensburg.[19]

The enterprise of theological dialog or "ecumenism" is always precarious. This was especially so in Contarini's day. William Anderson wrote two decades ago, "To be ecumenical in the middle of the 1980s is almost fashionable; in the sixteenth century it was a serious and often dangerous challenge."[20] This reality infused the work of Regensburg with apprehension.

---

16. William P. Anderson, "Gasparo Contarini: Sixteenth Century Ecumenist," *Ecumenical Trends* 13 (October 1984): 140.
17. J. Atkinson, "Martin Luther: Prophet to the Church Catholic," *Scottish Journal of Theology* 37 (1984): 316.
18. Peter Matheson, *Cardinal Contarini at Regensburg* (Oxford: Oxford Univ. Press, 1972), 93–94.
19. The colloquy also goes by the name Ratisbon. While the city where the conference was held was Regensburg, the Roman Catholic diocese to which that city belonged was named Ratisbon. For this reason Roman Catholic writers frequently (although not exclusively) use the name Ratisbon.
20. Anderson, "Gasparo Contarini," 140.

The Diet opened on April 5 with a solemn Mass of the Holy Spirit in St. Peter's Cathedral. With all the pomp and circumstance that one could expect, the procession wound its way by foot from the imperial quarters in the Golden Cross Inn to the church. The Protestants did not take part in the procession. Nor, surprisingly, did Contarini, though he did participate in the service. After the ceremony was finished, the colloquy participants met in the imperial chamber of the town hall to begin their meeting.[21]

The discussion centered on a book presented by Nicholas Granvelle, chancellor of Charles V, with the comment that it had been compiled by a group of Belgian theologians now deceased.[22] This was a lie. Actually, Gropper, Bucer, and a certain Gerhard Veltwyck had secretly composed it. In a series of twenty-three articles, principle points of theology were presented in a manner as agreeable to both sides as possible.[23]

After opening the Regensburg book and starting theological dialog, to the surprise of many, the groups achieved a considerable amount of agreement. The first four articles—dealing with the creation of humans and their state before the fall, free will, the cause of sin, and original sin—went uncontested and unchanged by both groups.[24]

On the next day, April 28, the controversial matter of justification was put on the table. Neither Eck nor Melanchthon was pleased with the "long-winded and highly ambiguous article."[25] Their insistence on its inadequacy caused the book to be put aside; instead they embarked

---

21. Matheson, *Cardinal Contarini*, 79–80.
22. An English version of the Regensburg book was made from the Latin almost immediately after the conference, but apparently it has not been reprinted since. An unknown library (located in Europe) has the original English manuscript. There are two microfilm copies: one is at the University of California library in Berkeley, and the other is in the Bodleian Library at Oxford. A translation was also made into German by Bucer.
23. Heinz Mackensen, "The Diplomatic Role of Gasparo Cardinal Contarini at the Colloquy of Ratisbon of 1541," *Church History* 27 (1958), 315.
24. Hans J. Hillerbrand, ed., *The Oxford Encyclopedia of the Reformation* (New York: Oxford Univ. Press, 1996), 377–78.
25. Matheson, *Cardinal Contarini*, 105.

upon an open discussion of the topic. Melanchthon initiated with an explanation of the Protestant position. The Catholics took issue with some of his terminology, and it was therefore rejected. Then on the following day, the Protestants, in turn, rejected the Catholic draft. Melanchthon suggested breaking off negotiations. In response Gropper and Pflug allowed the Protestants to revise the Catholic draft, which resulted in "agreement" on the doctrine of justification.[26]

An inside look at the Protestants' reaction to the Catholic concession is found in a personal letter of Calvin to his friend William Farel: "You will marvel when you read the copy of the article on justification ... that our adversaries have conceded so much. For they have committed themselves to the essentials of what is our true teaching. Nothing is to be found in it which does not stand out in our writings."[27]

Although conservative Catholics such as Eck were not pleased with the Protestant flavor of the article, there were some from the Catholic camp that approved. Among this group was Contarini. His confidant Reginald Pole, writing later to Contarini, "likened the formula to a partly concealed pearl, always possessed by the Church, but now accessible to everyone."[28]

In the midst of celebration there was skepticism on the part of the Protestants as to the truthfulness and sincerity of the Catholic agreement. Along with Melanchthon, Calvin was not convinced. He believed the Catholic side to be playing a political game. He contended, "The aim of the papal representatives remained now as before the reduction of the Protestants."[29]

---

26. Ibid., 107. The two main features of the justification article were an insistence that divine acceptance is by grace alone, not as a result of meritorious works, and second, the impossibility of separating faith from a practical outworking of love. In this way the statement was basic enough for both parties to embrace simply by extrapolating toward their respective positions. For a modern version of this statement, see the *Joint Declaration on the Doctrine of Justification* by the Lutheran World Federation and the Catholic Church.
27. Ibid., 142.
28. Wilhelm Schenk, *Reginald Pole, Cardinal of England* (London: Longmans, Green, and Co., 1950), 102.
29. Matheson, *Cardinal Contarini*, 113.

With agreement reached on the doctrine of justification, discussion continued on May 3 on the next section of the Regensburg book, dealing with the matter of the church and its authority. This is where fireworks erupted. Articles 6 through 8 were accepted with little dispute. Then came article 9. It dealt with the authority of the church in regard to Scripture.[30]

Like the previous statements, article 9 was framed in the most conciliatory terms. Reference to the teaching office of the papacy was deliberately excluded. Nevertheless, the statement asserted that God's Word was not only bound to Scripture but also to the dogmatic tradition of the church. Bucer, being the consummate diplomat, argued as a Protestant in favor of the Protestants' accepting the article. Melanchthon, however, was not able to overlook the difference so easily. For him, agreeing to elevate tradition to the place of Scripture would have meant betrayal of the Protestant cause. Since the issue was equally as important to the Roman Catholics, both sides became stuck in a doctrinal impasse. It was evident to all participants that the colloquy was in jeopardy of an irreparable conflict.

Count Fredrick of Palatinate proposed that the Protestant representatives submit their own statement as an alternative. "Like the original article, this Protestant draft was unpolemical, and went far to meet the Catholic position."[31] The interpretive role of the church was acknowledged, and based upon Augustine they agreed that Scripture was to be properly understood in the church. Nevertheless, the Protestants objected that the gift of interpreting Scripture was bound to any particular church office. They argued, "On historical, therefore, as well as theological grounds the infallibility of the Councils and of the early Church Fathers could not be accepted."[32]

In the face of an obvious stalemate, Granvelle intervened, calling for further discussion of article 9 to be postponed to the end of the colloquy. From the outside it may have appeared that the meeting

30. Ibid., 116.

31. Ibid., 118.

32. Ibid.

was progressing according to plan, but to insiders the severity of the impasse was obvious.

When the issue of authority was evaded, the doom of the colloquy seemed certain. Although the discussion continued further to address articles 10–17, on the sacraments, the dark cloud of article 9 loomed overhead. When it came to the matter of the Mass, Contarini departed from his normal friendly manner and dogmatically insisted on the use of the term *transubstantiation*. Another debate ensued. Historian Michael McDuffee explains why Contarini probably changed his attitude so drastically: "Contarini 'fast forwarded' failure's arrival by demanding that the Lord's elements must be understood in terms of transubstantiation. He probably did this to cover himself after the issue of authority made it clear that there would be no general agreement.... It is true no agreement over the nature of the real presence of Christ was reached; however, this was an anticlimactic conflict. Doctrinal differences receded in significance in comparison to the single most important question, 'who has the authority to pronounce on matters of doctrine?' This remains the most important point of division between Catholicism and Protestantism today."[33]

When it was time for Contarini to choose a side, he submitted to the authority with which he was most familiar. He was a Catholic, which was demonstrated by his choice of the papacy over his own conscience. On May 29 the colloquy ended, having lasted for about a month, while the imperial convention continued until July 29.[34] The conclusion of Contarini and the *Spirituali* is described by Oxford historian Diarmaid MacCulloch:

> Contarini had aroused many fears in Rome by his willingness to compromise, and he died under house arrest, a broken man, in August 1542. By then, the more confrontational *Spirituali* were alert to the danger of their position. De Valdes

33. Michael McDuffee, interview by author, 11 December 2000, Chicago, Illinois, electronic mail.

34. Mackensen, "Diplomatic Role," 316.

> avoided the testing time by his death in 1541, but Bernardo Ochino was summoned to Rome when his sermons became ever more outspoken. Sensibly disregarding the order, he had time to say good-bye to the dying Contarini before he left on horseback for Switzerland and Calvin's Geneva, and he was closely followed in his flight by Peter Martyr Vermigli, whose wanderings eventually took him to a warm welcome from Bucer in Strassburg. The sensation was huge at the flight of these preachers whom all Italy knew, and theirs were only the first in a series of defections of Italian scholars and theologians to the Reformed world across the Alps.[35]

The next decade of church history stands in stark contrast to the work of Contarini and other Catholic reformers. It was the era of inquisition, a time when the church accused proponents of renewal and other dissenters of heresy and treated them accordingly. Once accused, you were presumed guilty until proven otherwise; you were rarely confronted by your accusers; you could be made to testify against yourself, and you could be tortured. If sentenced, you faced imprisonment, loss of property, or burning at the stake, unless you confessed or recanted. Among the more prominent of these inquisitors was Cardinal Gian Pietro Carafa, later to be called Pope Paul IV. MacCulloch summarizes Carafa's legacy:

> Gian Pietro Carafa's hour had come. [He] had a cast-iron case to persuade Pope Paul III to set up a Roman Inquisition, modeled on the Spanish Inquisition, and with the cardinal-archbishop of Naples himself as one of the inquisitors-general. The papal Bull was promulgated on 21 July 1542. "Even if my own father were a heretic, I would gather the wood to burn him," Carafa vowed.[36]

---

35. MacCulloch, *The Reformation*, 224. Someone needs to write a comprehensive history of these Italian Evangelical preachers. If you're looking for a dissertation topic, it's waiting for you! Or maybe a monograph titled *Preachers Whom All of Italy Knew*. I triple-dog dare you!

36. Ibid.

> Carafa knew that his time was short, but his energy was undiminished and he worked fast. At last he had the power to put into effect the rigorous agenda that might be expected from the founder of the Roman Inquisition; he could treat the world with the same austere Puritanism that governed his own life (with the exception of his relatives, to whom he was almost as indulgent as any of his aristocratic Italian predecessors). It was during Paul IV's pontificate, in 1557, that the Roman Inquisition first issued a general Index of forbidden books for the whole Church.[37]

Carafa became Pope Paul IV, and his unpopular reputation, even among Catholics, preceded him. Reasons for this were numerous: he hated Spaniards and was an anti-Semite who confined Jews of the Papal States in ghettos and required them to wear distinctive yellow hats. His mafialike political shenanigans embarrassed the clergy, as did his scornful intolerance of anyone who crossed him.[38] Eventually, when Pope Paul IV breathed his last breath, "the news of his death in August 1559 sparked riotous celebrations; in Rome the crowd sacked the offices of the Inquisition to destroy their files, and to the north in Perugia there was a similar mob attack on the Church of Santo Domenico, which housed the local headquarters of the Inquisition."[39] Unfortunately, the damage was already done. The flame of renewal was doused and the organizational groundwork of a previous generation destroyed.

THREE TYPES OF CATHOLICS

Before concluding this chapter, we will revisit the question raised earlier concerning the basic Catholic profiles of the Reformation period. Hopefully, we now see how Luther represents the "ex-Catholic,"

37. Ibid., 269.
38. Ibid., 269–70.
39. Ibid., 270–71.

Ignatius the "traditional Catholic," and Contarini the "Evangelical Catholic." The key to recognizing this typology is the connection between these individuals and the particular religious authority to which they submitted. Because Luther rejected papal supremacy in favor of the biblical text, he represents Protestants. Because Ignatius and his followers went with the pope, the Jesuits characterize traditional Catholics. And since Contarini based his personal faith upon Scripture while also aligning with the papacy, he fits into the category of Evangelical Catholic. Each of these profiles, along with a fourth, the "cultural Catholic," will be taken up in part 2, where we consider the values and priorities of our Roman Catholic loved ones.

In the next chapter we will consider the fourth reason why many Catholics move in an Evangelical direction: a desire for Christ-centered devotion.

Chapter 7

REASON FOUR: CHRIST-CENTERED DEVOTION

Last night I sat on the family-room floor and watched the film *Angela's Ashes*. It is the autobiography of Frank McCourt, who describes his life in Ireland during the 1930s and 1940s. His family lived in a hovel with one bare lightbulb and bedbugs, and shared one outdoor toilet with all their neighbors. Because his dad was an alcoholic and seldom found work, McCourt's family subsisted on unemployment. For many painful years the family survived on just bread and tea.

In the early part of the film, McCourt's mother (Angela) loses her three babies, Margaret-Mary, Eugene, and Oliver, to "consumption," the dreaded disease which plagued the poor. As I sat with my heart glued to the screen, I wondered how the McCourts would draw from the resources of their Roman Catholic heritage to persevere through the dark valley of suffering. In various scenes the family appealed to God by means of candles, rosary beads, the saints, and sacramental rituals. It was striking to see how radically different this piety appeared compared with Evangelical prayer and worship.

Catholic devotion is enormous in scope and staggering in complexity, emerging from two thousand years of Christian faith and reflection. Such a tradition is arguably one of Roman Catholicism's greatest strengths, as many Protestants are quick to point out. In his book *Christian Spirituality*, Oxford historian Alister McGrath provides a helpful primer to the tradition, explaining how it provides guidance in the areas of reading, prayer, meditation, silence, study, and service. Such disciplines have enriched the church's spiritual vision for centuries and are part of the "Great Tradition" which is our common religious heritage. This tradition is now immensely popular among Evangelicals.

Usually, by the time an academic conversation reaches the church, it has become passe in the halls of education, but a current exception is the Great Tradition. Whether you peruse books for sale at the Evangelical Theological Society or visit the aisles at your local bookstore, you'll find a large collection of titles featuring key terms like *patristics*, *fathers*, *tradition*, or *rule of faith*. To be sure, some Evangelicals have written on the topic for years (for example, Richard J. Foster, Thomas Oden, Dallas Willard, and the late Robert Webber). Now, however, the proliferation of conferences, books, and blogs is in the mainstream, and it's bigger than ever. Evangelicals, it appears, are deeply interested in understanding the church before the sixteenth century.

When Evangelicals read the Bible, we don't ordinarily think about how our understanding of doctrine has been shaped by church history. We operate according to a certain assumption, which some have called the "ditch theory."[1] The figure on page 93 provides an explanation.

According to the theory, Jesus and the apostles understood and practiced Christian faith in all of its fullness and purity. This faithfulness continued until Emperor Constantine declared Christianity to be the official religion of the empire, at which time the church's purity fell into the ditch of compromise and heresy. From Constantine unto the medieval age, the gospel was immersed in unbiblical tradition and therefore was largely misunderstood by people apart from a small

1. I was introduced to this concept during college by Professor Gregg Quiggle in his class on church history.

THE "DITCH" THEORY OF CHURCH HISTORY

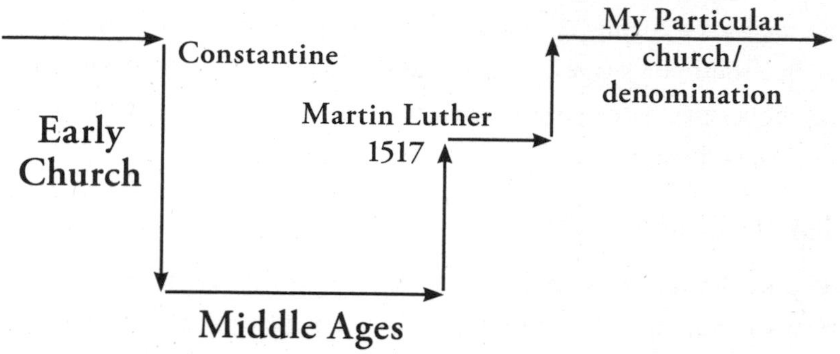

remnant of believers who somehow got it right. Eventually, in 1517 Martin Luther was raised up by God to confront these errors, which he initiated by nailing his ninety-five theses to the castle door at Wittenberg. With Luther and the Reformation, Christianity was brought three quarters of the way out of the ditch. In this almost-restored condition, Christianity remained until the founding of my particular denomination or church, at which time pure, biblical faith was finally returned to its original pristine condition.

To be sure, the ditch theory is a caricature, and yet its storyline is implicit in much Protestant teaching. As Tom Howard, a former Evangelical who is now a Catholic scholar, writes, "[Evangelicals] speak of the ancient faith as though the Bible had swum into view just this morning and as though one's approach to it is simply to open it, read, and start running."[2] Even if we disagree with the ditch theory in principle, we can't deny that it accurately describes much of our thinking and practice.

Recently, after a Sunday school class which explored historical events and ideas from the early church, a congregant asked me if I would ever recommend reading books from the Great Tradition (by which she meant works from a Roman Catholic or an Eastern Orthodox perspective). I told her how I purposefully expose myself to the

2. Thomas Howard, *On Being Catholic* (San Francisco: Ignatius, 1997), 224.

Great Tradition in three ways: *Touchstone* magazine, a catalog of classic works sold by Eighth Day Books, and *First Things* journal. She seemed a bit surprised that her Evangelical pastor would maintain such a routine. I suggested that reading books and articles from a different perspective can be tremendously worthwhile (assuming that one evaluates them in light of Scripture).[3]

BEWARE OF *NUDA SCRIPTURA*

Unlike the few Evangelicals who read about the creeds, spirituality, and worship of the early church, there are many in the Evangelical camp who have a visceral reaction against anything that goes by the name "tradition." This position, sometimes called *nuda Scriptura* (nude Scripture) removes tradition from the ongoing life of the church, insisting that the Bible function as the *only* source of authority for Christian faith and practice. While this definition may sound like what the Protestant Reformers meant by the term *sola Scriptura* (Scripture alone), it is actually quite different.

Evangelicals who hold this different position claim to operate apart from any form of church tradition. I once encountered this view at a Plymouth Brethren assembly. The marquee outside the building said, "No creed but the Bible." Upon entering, I picked up a monthly calendar which highlighted Sunday school classes, Wednesday night prayer, a weekly congregational hymn sing—practices that come from the Christian tradition but are not explicitly found in the Bible. I also noticed that the preacher quoted more than once from the founder of the Plymouth Brethren, a late-nineteenth-century Englishman named J. N. Darby. My Brethren friend was comfortable describing the Godhead in terms of the "Trinity" (a word that appears nowhere in Scripture), and if we had dialogued further, I'm sure he would have affirmed the hypostatic union or the Great Commission. With all due respect to my friend and the nice people of his assembly, it is

3. It also helps to be acquainted with historical theology to appreciate how religious thought is shaped in the context of human history.

somewhat misleading and less than biblical to suggest that Christians should (or even can) operate in a vacuum, apart from the influence of Christian tradition.[4]

I often think that the language of "Scripture alone" is unfortunate because at face value it sounds like Protestants are espousing the misnomer I just described. In actuality, we're trying to express what was essentially the concern of Jesus in Matthew 15:9 (compare with Isa. 19:13), where the Lord warns against presenting the "commandments of men" as God's Word, since such development of dogma may obscure or in some instances even contradict the teaching of Scripture. From an Evangelical point of view, this is how aspects of Catholic teaching like purgatory, indulgences, and Mary's co-mediation are viewed. Instead of serving divine revelation, these traditions threaten to undermine it.

I like how the late Harold O. J. Brown described the problem of *nuda Scriptura*: "If we consider faith as a climber trying to scale a snowy mountain peak, the one group [Catholics] will have him so packed in flowing garments that he can hardly move, while the other [Evangelicals] might have him naked and barefoot—or to be more decent, in shorts and sneakers—and in imminent danger of hypothermia."[5]

Unfortunately, when Catholics critique *sola Scriptura* (which is generally their chief contention), it is often the flawed view, what we're calling *nuda Scriptura*, that they go after. Although perhaps it's more troubling, from my perspective, when the same mistake is made by Evangelicals. (Since it's our doctrine, we should at least understand it.) When all is said and done, I agree with the conclusion of Brown, who says, "We need to accept tradition in principle, and at the same

4. On a subsequent occasion I discussed this concern with my friend. He argued that Jesus intended his followers to operate from the text alone, just as the Lord operated on the basis of the Hebrew Scriptures. Our conversation didn't last too much longer beyond my question about why the Lord attended synagogue when there's no mention of it in the Old Testament.

5. Harold O. J. Brown, *Reclaiming the Great Tradition*, ed. James S. Cutsinger (Downers Grove, IL: InterVarsity, 1997), 77.

time we need to be critical of traditions, both our own and those of others, lest they become the 'commandments of men' about which Jesus warns us."[6]

THE BODY OF CHRIST

Observing the large assortment of sacramental beads and bells in *Angela's Ashes*, I asked myself the question which passes through all Evangelicals' minds when they observe Catholic devotion: in what way do these practices relate to the person and work of Jesus? I see the saints. I see the rosary beads and hear prayers to Mary. I see examples of medieval mysticism and ethnic customs, like eating codfish during Lent. But how do these disciplines actually contribute to the worship of Jesus?

My concern is that the unintended result of so much Catholic tradition is that Jesus gets pushed into the background. In our research among ex-Catholics this tendency emerged as another reason for leaving the Catholic Church. In the words of one former Catholic, "When I acquired an understanding that Jesus alone is Lord, I became intolerant of rituals that divert attention from his supremacy." The rituals to which he referred were traditional practices which focus upon other religious objects or persons, such as Mary and the saints. To understand this tradition, we shall begin by asking, Why does it have such a varied and complex shape?

To start with, we must recognize that there is an essential difference in the way that Catholics and Protestants study God, the way we approach theology. Priests don't simply open their Bibles and concentrate all of their effort upon the study of Scripture before reaching a conclusion. For the Catholic, it is necessary to operate from the teaching that has developed over the course of Catholic history. This "rule of faith," or "Sacred Tradition" as it's called, is an authority binding the conscience of every faithful Catholic. In this way, the "Word of God" is not defined by Scripture alone (as Evangelicals would understand it); rather, God's Word is considered to be a combination of Scripture

6. Ibid., 85.

and tradition. In the words of the *Catechism*, "Sacred Tradition and Sacred Scripture make up a single sacred deposit of the 'Word of God' (*DV* 10), in which, as in a mirror, the pilgrim Church contemplates God, the source of all her riches."[7]

The reason why Catholics understand tradition to possess divine authority may be summarized in one word: incarnation. Most Christians have probably used or have at least heard the term. It's a word that surfaces often during the Advent and Christmas seasons. The incarnation describes the great event in which the second person of the triune God became flesh. On this much Catholics and Evangelicals agree—born of a virgin, Jesus of Nazareth is fully God and fully man. However, in Catholic thought, the term *incarnation* has additional meaning.

The critical difference between Catholics and Evangelicals concerns the relationship of Jesus' incarnation to his church. In what St. Augustine and later theologians called the "total Christ" (*totus Christus*) the incarnated presence of Jesus (the head) is manifested in his church (the members) to make up the body of Christ.[8] Accordingly, incarnation is not simply a historical event from two millennia ago; it is also an ongoing mystical process that applies to his body.[9] The late Father Yves Congar (a key voice from Vatican II) put it this way: "Since the medieval era ... we have witnessed a particular fondness for St. Augustine's formula, 'the whole Christ,' or for the formula of St. Joan of Arc, 'I think that between our Lord and the Church—it is all one,' ... or for the theme of 'continuing incarnation.'"[10]

7. *Catechism of the Catholic Church*, para. 97.
8. Émilien Lamirande, *The Communion of Saints*, trans. A. Manson (New York: Hawthorn, 1963), 73.
9. Joseph Cardinal Ratzinger, *Principles of Catholic Theology: Building Stones for Fundamental Theology*, trans. Sr. Mary Frances McCarthy, S.N.D. (San Francisco: Ignatius, 1987), 44–47, 245.
10. Yves Congar, O.P., *Jesus Christ*, trans. Luke O'Neill (New York: Herder and Herder, 1965), 156–57. Also in the *Catechism of the Catholic Church*: "The Church is both visible and spiritual, a hierarchical society and the Mystical Body of Christ. She is one, yet formed of two components, human and divine. That is her mystery, which only faith can accept.... The Church in this world is the sacrament of salvation, the sign and the instrument of the communion of God and men" (*Catechism of the Catholic Church*, para. 779–80).

In effect, the Catholic position says that if you want to see Jesus in the world, look to the Roman Catholic Church. This is why Big Joe, the deacon from my childhood parish whom I referenced earlier, pointed to the Catholic sacraments as the place where one receives life in Christ. The institution of the church is considered to be the embodiment of Jesus on earth (Congar's point with the language of "continuing incarnation"). To come to Christ, one must come to the church; they are the same entity, just as a head and a body make up a single person.[11] To understand the crux of the issue, consider the following analogy.

THE GREAT SYMPHONY

Occasionally a congregant will give me tickets to a classical music concert. Such performances are impressive when you think that an orchestra of so many individuals playing different instruments can produce such a rhythmically coherent sound. It works because these musicians rely on two crucial ingredients: a score, which explains the notes to play, and a conductor, who provides personal direction. It would be catastrophic if the orchestra tore up the score or eliminated the conductor.

An even more amazing fact is that two orchestras playing from identical scores can sound so different. When Arturo Toscanini conducted Haydn's Oratorio *The Creation* at La Scala, he did so with the punctilious style for which he was famous. Leonard Bernstein, on the other hand, conducted this piece in Vienna as only someone with his eccentric personality could. They presented the same score in a different style, which resulted in a different orchestral sound. The same principle applies to worship.

It is appropriate to expect variety and creativity in the Christian tradition. God, who exists in three persons, relating to millions of different people in diverse cultures and time periods will naturally generate a rich collection of religious experience. Such divine activity should

11. Lamirande, *Communion of Saints*, 75.

be recognized and celebrated, for it bears witness to the wonder of a God who relates personally to his creation. Having come from an Evangelical background, Thomas Howard is well acquainted with this dynamic: "Surely this riotous fructifying of fashions in public worship suggests something deeply significant about the gospel, namely, that it is a seed of such glorious vitality that, when it is planted anywhere among us mortals, it will sprout, burgeon, and bear good fruit. And more: in the colorful heaps displayed in this harvest we find the rich and particular genius of each tribe and people, redeemed, purified, raised, and touched with eternity itself. What you find in Spain and Latin America differs greatly from what you find in the Netherlands or Norway. Sicilians do not order their worship as do the Watutsi; nor does Irish Catholicism yield just the look given things by the Filipinos."[12]

As Howard describes, we should expect for there to be differences of style in public worship depending on one's context. If you doubt this, find a missionary in your church who is home on furlough, take him or her out to lunch, and ask for a description of the worship style of the people among whom he or she serves. Variety is a good thing. However, we must remember that while Toscanini and Bernstein differed in their presentations of Haydn's score, the broad outline remained fundamentally the same. In "The Heavens Are Telling," the woodwinds carry the melody. Occasionally, the melody is accented by the horns, but the two instruments are never confused. If either conductor failed to differentiate between the horns and the woodwinds, the integrity of Haydn's famous chorus would have been compromised. Herein is the concern that Evangelicals have with Roman Catholic devotion. The horn of tradition frequently seems to usurp the woodwinds of Scripture. Let me give you an example.

RELIGIOUS DISSONANCE

A year ago I acquired a penchant for Relevant Radio, a Roman Catholic radio station broadcasting in the Chicagoland area which provides

12. Howard, *On Being Catholic*, 34.

thought-provoking dialog, commentary, and call-in segments. These programs have been enormously helpful during research for this book because much of their discussion deals with the Catholic faith applied by lay listeners. I especially enjoy listening to a priest named Father John Corapi.

After several decades of tremendous wealth followed by severe poverty, Father Corapi eventually dedicated himself to the priesthood and was ordained by Pope John Paul II. His teaching is trenchantly orthodox, emphasizing fidelity to Catholic doctrine as taught by the Catholic catechism. The Corapi website describes his ministry with these words: "The essence of Father's message is the essential message of Jesus Christ. It is Good News: a message of truth and goodness, love and mercy. It is above all else a message of hope."[13]

Notice how the summary of Father Corapi's ministry begins with an emphasis on "the essential message of Jesus Christ." This statement is consistent with what you find in Catholic teaching. Whether it is in the *Catechism*, the writing of Pope Benedict XVI (particularly expositions like his book *Jesus of Nazareth*), or the teaching of Catholic bishops, Jesus is the explicit starting point and aspiration of faith. Unfortunately, what begins with a Christ-centered focus often veers off in another direction.

Recently, while listening to Father Corapi, he made the following statements. Since I was driving on the highway at the time (and have never learned how to write shorthand), what you read is a paraphrase: "You can't stare directly at the sun, but you can look at the moon. Mary, the Mother of God, is like the moon reflecting the luminous glory of the Son. If you want to approach the Lord Jesus Christ, go to the Mother of God; bring your requests to his mother, and she will bring you to her son. After all, what Jewish boy could ever refuse the request of his mother?"

Later in the message, Father Corapi explained with much earnestness how to promote Christian spirituality. In his words:

---

13. *www.fathercorapi.com.*

Do you want to be a spiritual person? There are three things you need to do.

1. Maintain devotion to Mary.
2. Spend an hour each day before the Blessed Sacrament, the Eucharist.
3. Be lockstep with the magisterium (the official teaching of Rome).

In keeping with the principle of continuing incarnation, Jesus is identified as the center and circumference of Catholic faith, but in practice, Sacred Tradition asserts Mary, the sacraments, or some other aspect of magisterial teaching, to the extent that Jesus inadvertently slips from the picture.

Another example of this tendency: on November 30, 2007, at St. Peter's in Rome, Pope Benedict XVI issued the second encyclical of his pontificate. *Spe salvi*, "Saved by Hope," is a thoughtful and stimulating document. It begins with the following words: "*Spe Salvi facti sumus*—in hope we were saved, says Saint Paul to the Romans, and likewise to us (Rom. 8:24). According to the Christian faith, 'redemption'—salvation—is not simply a given. Redemption is offered to us in the sense that we have been given hope, trustworthy hope, by virtue of which we can face our present: the present, even if it is arduous, can be lived and accepted if it leads towards a goal, if we can be sure of this goal, and if this goal is great enough to justify the effort of the journey."

The great biblical scholar that he is, Pope Benedict XVI starts by referencing Paul's declaration on hope to the Romans. The encyclical continues to assemble some of the strongest statements of Scripture on the topic. He also cites some excellent passages from the church fathers and interacts with an impressive range of modern thinkers, from Bacon and Kant to Marx and Adorno. From the table of contents you get a bird's eye view of the document:[14]

---

14. Ignatius Press has published *Spe salvi* in a book titled *Saved in Hope* (San Francisco: Ignatius, 2007).

- Introduction
- Faith is hope
- The concept of faith-based hope in the New Testament and the early Church
- Eternal life—what is it?
- Is Christian hope individualistic?
- The transformation of Christian faith—hope in the modern age
- The true shape of Christian hope
- "Settings" for learning and practicing hope

    1. Prayer as a school of hope
    2. Action and suffering as settings for learning hope
    3. Judgment as a setting for learning and practicing hope

- Mary, Star of Hope

Spe salvi is worth reading. In his classic fashion, the pope doesn't simply teach the Great Tradition; he masterfully applies its truth to our contemporary world with the incisive and prophetic voice we have come to expect of him. For instance, consider his words from paragraph 16: "How did we arrive at this interpretation of the 'salvation of the soul' as a flight from responsibility for the whole, and how did we come to conceive the Christian project as a selfish search for salvation which rejects the idea of serving others?"

I salute the pope for statements like this. We, the church, must humbly respond to such exhortations if we're serious about showing the world true hope. At the same time, there are some places in the encyclical where Evangelical readers will have difficulty. The pope shadow boxes with Luther's understanding of faith (para. 7), assumes infant baptism to be the normative means of regeneration (para. 10), and reflects on the significance of purgatory (para. 44–47). The most disturbing part may very well be the concluding section, in which the pope prayerfully extols Mary as a "Star of Hope": "Thus you remain in the midst of the disciples as their Mother, as the Mother of hope.

Holy Mary, Mother of God, our Mother, teach us to believe, to hope, to love with you. Show us the way to his kingdom! Star of the Sea, shine upon us and guide us on our way!"[15]

My reason for quoting the pope is simply to illustrate how, in the final analysis, aspects of Sacred Tradition can eclipse the Christ-centered message of Scripture. I now write this on a Monday during Advent. Yesterday morning in the worship services of College Church I read from Luke's gospel about the piety of Jesus' mother, Mary. We eagerly join our voices with the Great Tradition in thankfulness for and admiration of the humble and faithful girl whose soul magnified the Lord. But on the basis of Scripture, Evangelicals maintain that Jesus—the Star of Hope—is the one intermediary between God and humanity, the Savior, whom we exalt, who alone shines redemptive light into our hearts (2 Cor. 4:6; 1 Tim. 2:5).

■■■

Of the five reasons for leaving Roman Catholicism, the one covered in the next chapter is probably the most prominent. When participants in our focus groups spoke of it, they did so with remarkable passion and specificity. It is, simply put, the desire to be motivated by grace instead of guilt.

15. A similar movement from Scripture to exaltation of Mary is found in the tenth encyclical of Pope John Paul II, *Veritatis splendor* [The Splendor of Truth].

Chapter 8

REASON FIVE: MOTIVATED BY GRACE INSTEAD OF GUILT

A parish deacon blesses and lights the Paschal candle. You've seen this candle before; it's the tall white one with the cross in the middle and brass helmet on top. Depending on the time of year, it stands beside the altar or near the baptismal font. This particular occasion was the Easter vigil, and as is customary, the deacon chanted the so-called Exultet (Easter proclamation) in his resonant baritone voice. So beautiful are the words that they're worth reading:

Accept this Easter candle,
a flame divided but undimmed,
a pillar of fire that glows to the honor of God.
Let it mingle with the lights of heaven
and continue bravely burning
to dispel the darkness of this night!
May the Morning Star which never sets
find this flame still burning:
Christ, that Morning Star,
who came back from the dead,

and shed his peaceful light on all humanity,
your Son, who lives and reigns for ever and ever.
Amen.

The Paschal candle remains lit during Mass throughout the Easter season. Since it symbolizes the life of Christ, it is used in baptismal services to portray spiritual birth. As I observed the service of a friend's newborn daughter, I was intrigued by the rich use of symbols and wondered if anyone else appreciated the theological lessons being displayed before us.

My friends carried precious little Charlotte to the baptismal font in her white, multilayered, lacy fabric dress, swaddled in a blanket which had been knitted by someone's great-grandmother and passed down through the generations. Gathered around were family members, godparents, close friends, and a priest. The priest signed Charlotte with the cross in what Catholics call the "imprint of Christ." After reading Scripture, the priest then anointed her forehead, lips, throat, and chest with holy oil, symbolizing the Holy Spirit's presence and protection over her. He blessed the baptismal water and poured some of it over her head while saying, "Charlotte, I baptize you in the name of the Father and of the Son and of the Holy Spirit." Perfumed oil was then applied to symbolize the Spirit's illumination. Godparents stood nearby holding their candles. With the flame from the Paschal candle before them, they spoke on behalf of Charlotte, affirming doctrinal beliefs and reciting the Lord's Prayer. The service concluded when the priest offered a solemn blessing.

This is how infants enter the Catholic Church, the first of seven such sacraments that will nurture Charlotte's soul with saving grace. These sacraments are:

1. Baptism
2. Penance
3. Eucharist
4. Confirmation
5. Anointing of the sick

The other two sacraments are equally significant, but not directly applicable to all Catholics:

6. Marriage (some Catholics remain single)[1]
7. Holy orders (only men can be ordained)

The seven sacraments of the Catholic Church are not liturgical options for religious overachievers. They are the heart of Catholic faith and practice. Not only do they mark the transitional stages of one's life, they are intended to empower one to remain in God's favor "from the womb to the tomb." If you want to understand what Catholics believe about salvation, you must be familiar with the sacraments. Therefore, we'll take a moment to consider them in turn.

After being baptized, the next step for Charlotte will be her First Holy Communion. This usually happens at age seven (before which time children are not held morally responsible for their sins). Little girls appear like miniature brides in white dresses, and boys traditionally wear white suits, white ties, and white shoes. (Keeping boys clean until after the service and the taking of photographs requires nothing short of a miracle.) It is immediately preceded by the sacrament of reconciliation (popularly known as confession). Traditionally, this has involved personal reflection on one's wrongdoings before admitting them to a priest, initiated with the words, "Bless me, Father, for I have sinned." In response, the priest assigns some form of penance, which is prayer or acts of service required of the penitent to make amends for their guilt.

Because the Eucharist is central to Catholic spiritual life, First Holy Communion is a milestone event. From that day forward, Charlotte will join her parish in a sacred meal that unites her to Christ and joins the members of the church to one another. On account of what Catholics call the "real presence" of Christ in the meal, they not only celebrate Jesus' sacrifice but also understand the Eucharist to infuse

1. The sacrament of marriage differs from the others in that rather than being officiated by the priest, the wedding ceremony is conducted by the (validly baptized) man and woman.

sanctifying grace into their souls. This is what makes Communion the "source and summit" of Catholic worship.[2]

The next sacramental ceremony in Charlotte's life will be confirmation. Usually at the time of life when a young person is beginning adolescence, it increases and further establishes the faith which has been initiated in baptism. (Local bishops decide the precise age of confirmation, which can be anywhere between seven and eighteen.) Any of us who have a vague recollection of what our adolescent years were like can understand why this would be important. Charlotte will choose a confirmation name, probably of a saint who is a spiritual example, and select a sponsor to stand up with her during the ceremony as a sign of support. Through the seven gifts of the Holy Spirit (wisdom, understanding, discernment, reverence, knowledge, courage, and holy fear), Charlotte seeks to receive spiritual empowerment before heading into adulthood.

Many years down the road, hopefully after Charlotte has lived a long and fruitful life, she will observe what is called anointing of the sick or last rites. Before Vatican II the church commonly referred to this practice as extreme unction. (Extreme describes the urgent condition of those about to depart from life, and unction refers to oil that is applied in the ritual.) Last rites involves three different sacraments in one: reconciliation, Eucharist, and anointing of the sick. All three are applied in one visit as a final infusion of sanctifying grace to cleanse and empower one who is about to cross the eternal threshold of death.

EX-CATHOLICS TALK ABOUT SALVATION

Our focus groups identified several factors that precipitated their departure from the Catholic Church. Among them, the chief reason, hands down, was disagreement with the Catholic way of salvation. When ex-Catholics communicated this idea, they often expressed appreciation for the rich symbolism, historical rootedness, and theo-

2. *Catechism of the Catholic Church*, para. 1324.

logical depth of Catholic rituals. At the same time, there was frustration and even resentment that one had spent decades in the Catholic Church without ever having heard a clear explanation of the salvation message. They understood how to obtain a relationship with the Catholic Church, but not with Jesus Christ.

We certainly don't want to drive a wedge between knowing Jesus and participating in his church. Evangelicals tend to make this tragic mistake. We absolutely need the community of God's people, for that is an essential part of our identity in Christ. The problem arises, however, when the Catholic Church postures herself as the sacramental mediator who alone represents Jesus Christ on earth. This position easily degenerates into relationship with the church institution instead of relationship with the person of Christ. Following is an example of how radically different these two approaches can be. It's the conversion story of a former Catholic, Andy Brucato, who now serves as an Evangelical missionary in northern Italy.

> This "good news" of salvation by faith, and not by rules-keeping, was unknown to me as a Catholic child growing up in the Bronx. Back then my life was fairly simple: school every day, kids' games in the neighborhood, and hot summers on the New York streets. Although life was not very complicated, I created my own confusion by starting to use drugs as a teenager. There was emptiness in my life that needed to be filled, but I did not know how. I enlisted in the Navy in 1968 and was sent to Vietnam. After the war, I returned to life in New York and to increased drug use. I was without direction and did not even know it.
>
> Then something changed. A friend of mine seemed to disappear from our little band of hippies. He was gone for about six months. When he returned, he said something had taken place in his life. He could not quite explain what had happened, but he gave me a Bible and asked me to start reading it.

> I left New York shortly afterwards and headed to Florida. I worked when I wanted to and played the rest of the time. I had no responsibilities and no ties. Inside, however, there was this emptiness that could not be filled with pleasure or drugs of the "free life." It was during that time that a middle-aged couple living near my home invited me to an Evangelical church to hear what the Bible said about future events. I heard not only about the future according to the Bible but also about my personal life and future. For the first time in my life I heard how much God loved me and how he had given his Son, Jesus Christ, to die in my place. I heard that he died for my sin, my drug abuse, my selfishness, and rose victoriously from the grave.
>
> The message was one that described not a new religion or a new set of rules but a relationship with the living God, who loved me and died for my sin and shame. This was the message I had longed for without even knowing it. The emptiness and void in my life was filled by the person of Christ himself. I accepted him as my Savior. It was the great exchange. I gave him my sin, and he gave me eternal life and forgiveness.
>
> I was keenly aware of the need of others to hear the good news of salvation through a personal relationship with the Lord Jesus. I wanted to share that news with all who would listen. My family and friends needed to hear that eternal life was a gift to be received, not a reward to be earned by good deeds or religious observances.[3]

If we were to unpack the elements of Andy's testimony, we'd find that they consist of ideas shared by most ex-Catholics. He mentions that his childhood experience of Catholicism was defined mainly by rules. Because rules fail to meet the longing of the human heart, his soul was left empty. This condition persisted until one day he

3. From email communication with Rev. Andy Brucato, 7 July 2008.

heard the message that Jesus died upon the cross as his substitute and rose victoriously from the grave, what he called the "great exchange." Unlike his rules-oriented experience of the Catholic Church, Andy now enjoyed a personal relationship with Christ by faith. This not only provided assurance that God had accepted him as a son; it also gave his life purpose in the enterprise of sharing the good news of Christ with others.

Andy's encounter with God is not only common to ex-Catholics; it's also the driving force behind their spiritual migration. As many of them explain it, "Instead of religion, I now have a relationship with God." Perhaps you've used this expression. If so, you know that it doesn't aim to denigrate religion as such. After all, Scripture uses the word *religion* positively. (James 1:27: "Religion that God our Father accepts as pure and faultless is this: to look after orphans and widows.") Rather, the contrast of religion and relationship underscores the fact that it's not necessary for one to first get right with the Catholic Church by observing sacramental stipulations before receiving salvation from Christ. Rather, it comes by faith alone. According to the apostle Paul, "If you confess with your mouth, 'Jesus is Lord,' and believe in your heart that God raised him from the dead, you will be saved. For it is with your heart that you believe and are justified, and it is with your mouth that you confess and are saved" (Rom. 10:9–10; see also Eph. 1:13–14). Or as the apostle Peter put it, "Everyone who calls on the name of the Lord will be saved" (Acts 2:21). Simply put, humanity is made right with God by believing in the gospel and not by meriting God's favor through sacred rituals.

Andy's testimony and others like it present an interesting irony. After individuals leave the Catholic Church, they regard the sacraments—the most important practices of the church and means of saving grace—as obstacles to genuine faith. From a Catholic point of view, this notion not only sounds ludicrous, it feels like an attack on one's church. It then takes about a nanosecond of thought before this threat becomes personal. Is it any wonder that Catholics often feel like they are put on the defensive by ex-Catholic Evangelicals?

Perhaps you're thinking, "Chris, you're making this stuff up. How could anyone raised in the Catholic Church not understand the gospel? Maybe a handful of people in your focus groups felt this way, but surely most Catholics don't." More than once I've had Catholic friends express this sort of skepticism. It's a fair response. For their sake, let me offer another example.

America is a national Catholic weekly magazine published by the Jesuits. In January of 1991 it ran an article titled "Coming to Grip with Losses: The Migration of Catholics into Conservative Protestantism" by Mark Christensen. The article is worth reading in its entirety. Below is an excerpt in which the author explains how the gospel remained obscure to him despite his years of active participation in the Catholic Church:

> The effect of the obscurity for me was that, while I certainly grew up knowing about Jesus, I never realized who He is or why He came to earth in the first place. I knew Catholicism.... I have been shaped by Catholicism as a religious system and culture—but, I never heard the Gospel.
>
> I can just see Catholic religious leaders pulling their hair out at that statement: "What do you mean you never heard the Gospel! What do you think we've been proclaiming the last 2,000 years in the Eucharist?" Yes, I realize the preeminent place Christ holds in the Mass. I know Scriptures are read every Sunday. I know the magnificence and purity of the Nicene Creed.... I've no interest in slandering an institution for which I hold tremendous respect. I have to report, though, what I hear coming from the mouth of ex-Catholics as they describe their number one reason for leaving Catholicism: "How could it be that I spent 22 years in the Catholic Church," one friend spoke angrily, "and never heard the Gospel?"

What Are the Real Issues Here?

> At first I wondered if we defectors weren't buying into a new spirituality as much as a new terminology when we left Catholicism. Maybe Evangelicals just had a prettier package on the same truths. But I tell you that I have asked dozens of Catholics in the last eight years if they know who Christ is or why He came to earth. Overwhelmingly they just don't know. I'm not talking about fundamentalist lingo here. I'm talking about the great apostolic message, uncluttered by jargon and qualification: Christ came to free us from the encumbrance of sin, providing us with what we could not do for ourselves: restore us to God for eternity.[4]

In March of that same year, *America* published a follow-up to Christensen's article because, in the editor's words, it "elicited many heated responses, both pro and con." What a surprise! The raw emotion of these rejoinders further illustrates the controversial nature of discussion of salvation between Catholics and Evangelicals.

To understand how exactly the Catholic and Evangelical positions on salvation differ, one must examine a few key issues. These include the perpetual sacrifice of the Mass, justification, works of supererogation, purgatory, indulgences, the treasury of merit, transubstantiation, the canons of the Council of Trent, the mediating role of Mary, imputation, penance, and clericalism. However, my editor (who has slightly bigger biceps than me) won the arm-wrestling match which decided that instead of addressing all of these topics, which would make our book twice as long, I would direct readers to another book. So here it is: *Roman Catholics and Evangelicals: Agreements and Differences* by Norman L. Geisler and Ralph E. MacKenzie. In my humble opinion it is the clearest and most thorough treatment of these issues. Not only does it address all of the topics I've mentioned, it does so with charity and insight.

---

4. Mark Christensen, "Coming to Grips with Losses: The Migration of Catholics into Conservative Protestantism," *America*, 26 January 1991, 58–59.

Before we conclude this chapter we must consider a practical implication that naturally emerges from the Catholic way of salvation. Regardless of one's age, location, or ethnic background, this factor exerts enormous influence upon the way ex-Catholics view God and salvation. It is an unhealthy guilt which questions whether we truly are accepted by God.

THE CENTRALITY OF GRACE

Imagine. You are at Spark's Steakhouse in New York for dinner on a Friday night. Since it's during the season of Lent, beef of any kind is prohibited. Your host insists that you order the steak tenderloin with mustard-cognac sauce, because it's the chef's specialty. What do you do?

At once, your Catholic conscience sends you into a tailspin. To consider eating meat on a Lenten Friday is a venial sin, and *wanting* to eat it is another one. You haven't opened the menu and you've already committed two sins. Your waiter delivers your beverages and says that he will return in a moment for your order. In the meantime, you wonder, "What if I ask for the steak?" Would this constitute a venial or mortal sin? It all depends. If you think it's mortal, it may very well be. If you think it's venial, it still could be mortal. By this point the waiter returns. He greets the host by name, looks at you, and with a genteel accent says, "May I suggest the steak tenderloin with mustard-cognac sauce?" You quickly decide that on this occasion at least, eating steak can't be more than a venial sin, and therefore respond, "I'll try it." Although you freely made this choice, you figure you can go to confession within twenty-four hours before the Saturday evening Mass. But does a venial sin become mortal when it's freely chosen? That's the risk you're taking. What if you mistakenly thought it was Thursday instead of Friday? This would allow you to eat meat, but, unfortunately, forgetting it was a Friday of Lent would be a sin. How about if you remembered it was Friday after your second forkful? Is it a venial sin to continue eating? If you feign a stomach ache and don't finish it, would lying then be a sin? Within ten minutes you've committed so many sins that your visit to purgatory has been extended by fifteen years.[5]

While this story is fictitious, the problem that it illustrates is all too real. If you grew up Catholic, you understand that guilt is not simply an incident; it is a form of psychosis. Over time it shapes one's mental hardware to the extent that impulses of guilt prevail.

In the genuinely funny book *Growing Up Catholic*, written by several Catholic authors, there's a segment called "The Great Guilt Contest: The Catholics and the Jews." Maybe because I'm a Long Islander who grew up surrounded by both, I resonate with it. Regardless of where you're from, you'll find that it contains a profound insight concerning the problem of guilt:

> In the contest for the Guilt Championship of the World, the undisputed co-champions are the Catholics and the Jews. Protestant work-ethic guilt, while a contender, just isn't in the same league. Although Catholic guilt and Jewish guilt may appear to be similar, they actually have very different origins. Jewish guilt is generally induced by the Jewish family after the violation of a cultural tradition, such as refusing to take home the extra chicken soup your mother made for you, or becoming a forest ranger instead of a doctor.
>
> Catholic guilt may be related to family disapproval as well, but not in such an immediate sense. The root of all Catholic guilt is the knowledge that every sin committed—past, present, or future—adds to Jesus' suffering on the cross. Since virtually anything you do (or don't do) may be a sin, this is a very heavy burden to bear. It's bad enough that you have to pay for sins yourself, but making the Nicest Guy Ever take the rap also is just too awful.

---

5. Inspiration for this illustration came from *Growing Up Catholic*, in which the authors describe a similar scenario involving a hotdog (Mary Jane Frances Cavolina Meara, Jeffrey Allen Joseph Stone, Maureen Anne Teresa Kelly, Richard Glen Michael Davis, *Growing Up Catholic* [Garden City, NY: Dolphin, 1984], 123–24).

> Thus the two outstanding forms of guilt may be summed up as follows. The wayward Jew thinks, "What an awful thing to do to somebody." The Catholic sinner thinks, "What an awful person I am."[6]

In fairness to the Catholic Church, she distinguishes between guilt, which is feeling bad about your behavior, and shame, which is directed at oneself. But when you spend your entire religious life saying *Mea culpa, mea culpa, mea maxima culpa* (Latin for "my fault, my fault, my most grievous fault") with a universe of religious stipulations waiting to be violated—everything from dietary regulations to holy days of obligation—it's not long before guilt grows into unmanageable proportions. It's like an iron bear-trap gripping your conscience; you either sever your conscience or remain captive to it.[7]

I believe that victory over unhealthy guilt follows from an understanding of who we are in Christ. After several years of my walking with Jesus, God used Galatians 2:20 to instill this lesson, particularly the words, "It is no longer I who live, but Christ who lives in me" (ESV). Furthermore, a lesson from the ministry of Luther called the "Dung Hill" also provided my Catholic conscience with liberation. Maybe you'll find it helpful too.

Supposedly, Martin Luther was sitting down with some of his students beside a window when snow started to fall. Luther pointed to a pile of manure near his house and explained to students that on account of sin, the moral condition of humans resembles the stinking pile of dung. Among the implications of this condition are guilt and condemnation before God.

Within the hour, snow had fallen so steadily that the dung hill was covered. Luther paused from his lesson and once again pointed to the mound. He asked the students to tell him what they saw. Instead of manure the students described a powdery white hill. As the sunlight

6. Ibid.

7. Instead of the options of a seared or severed conscience, God intends for his children to renew their minds by prayerfully and worshipfully filling themselves with biblical truth concerning his divine mercy and grace (Rom. 12:1–2).

gleamed off the fresh snow, Luther stated, "That is how God sees us in his Son, Jesus Christ. While we remain full of sin, in Christ we are clothed with his perfect righteousness and therefore we are acceptable in God's sight."

Every time I share this story, I quickly point out that the analogy is flawed. Because God provides his Holy Spirit and accomplishes his work of sanctification in us, he makes us more than dung. (Praise God!) This is where the analogy breaks down the most. But there's another part of the analogy that is not only accurate; it's glorious. It's what Andy Brucato, in his testimony, called the "great exchange"; namely, we give Christ our sin, and he gives us his righteousness. The idea is summarized nicely by the sixteenth-century English theologian Richard Hooker: "Such we are in the sight of God the Father, as is the very Son of God himself. Let it be counted folly or frenzy or fury or whatsoever. It is our wisdom and our comfort; we care for no knowledge in the world but this, that man has sinned and God has suffered; that God has made himself the sin of men, and that men are made the righteousness of God."[8]

Because our identity is founded in the resurrected Christ, who is seated at God's right hand, God looks upon us as being clothed with the perfection of his Son. On *this* basis, we are accepted, as Paul asserts in Romans 8:31–39:

> What, then, shall we say in response to this? If God is for us, who can be against us? He who did not spare his own Son, but gave him up for us all—how will he not also, along with him, graciously give us all things? Who will bring any charge against those whom God has chosen? It is God who justifies. Who is he that condemns? Christ Jesus, who died—more than that, who was raised to life—is at the right hand of God and is also interceding for us. Who shall separate us from the love of Christ? Shall trouble or hardship or persecution

8. Richard Hooker, "Sermon on Habakkuk 1:4" (1585), in *The Works of Richard Hooker*, ed. John Keble, vol. 3, 5th ed. (Oxford: Oxford Univ. Press, 1865), 490–91.

> or famine or nakedness or danger or sword? As it is written: "For your sake we face death all day long; we are considered as sheep to be slaughtered." No, in all these things we are more than conquerors through him who loved us. For I am convinced that neither death nor life, neither angels nor demons, neither the present nor the future, nor any powers, neither height nor depth, nor anything else in all creation, will be able to separate us from the love of God that is in Christ Jesus our Lord.

Paul's words not only provide the antidote to guilt; they also provide a healthy measure of assurance that in Christ we are fully accepted by God as his children. As Paul states earlier in Romans 5:8 – 10: "But God demonstrates his own love for us in this: While we were still sinners, Christ died for us. Since we have now been justified by his blood, how much more shall we be saved from God's wrath through him! For if, when we were God's enemies, we were reconciled to him through the death of his Son, how much more, having been reconciled, shall we be saved through his life!"

In addition to these great passages, there are four others that I would recommend internalizing if you continue to struggle with guilt. You might simply write them down on index cards and look at them in the spare moments of your day.

> *Psalm 103:12*: "As far as the east is from the west, so far has he removed our transgressions from us."
>
> *Romans 8:1*: "Therefore, there is now no condemnation for those who are in Christ Jesus."
>
> *Galatians 2:20*: "I have been crucified with Christ and I no longer live, but Christ lives in me. The life I live in the body, I live by faith in the Son of God, who loved me and gave himself for me."
>
> *2 Corinthians 5:21*: "God made him who had no sin to be sin for us, so that in him we might become the righteousness of God."

"IT IS FINISHED!"

I once taught a lesson at College Church titled "Why I Believe in Purgatory." If you ever want to draw large numbers of people to hear you speak and don't mind a lot of emails in your inbox beforehand, you should consider using it. The facial expressions of those sitting in the class before I started to speak were priceless. It was like the boy who looked up at Joe Jackson after the famous White Sox player was found guilty of fixing the 1919 World Series and exclaimed, "Say it ain't so, Joe." Many evidently thought that it would be my theological coming out party—true confessions of a closet Catholic. It probably didn't help that I started the lesson stating, "I believe in purgatory."

Toward the end of the lesson my wife glared at me as if to say, "*Please*, stop keeping these people in suspense." To avoid having to sleep on the couch that night, I decided that it was time to explain myself. My comments went something like the following:

> Some of you are wondering how it is I can believe in purgatory. Let me tell you. The word *purgatory* describes purification or purging from sin. In the Roman Catholic tradition this is believed to happen after people die in order for them to enter heaven spotless and pure. I also believe in purgatory; however, I believe that it happened once and for all on the cross of Jesus Christ. When the Lord hung between heaven and earth and shed his blood, he did so as a substitute for humanity. He paid the penalty for our guilt once and for all, even as it says in 1 Peter 3:18: "For Christ died for sins once for all, the righteous for the unrighteous, to bring you to God. He was put to death in the body but made alive by the Spirit."
>
> In his death Jesus perfectly satisfied the righteous requirement of God's law, which is why he says in John 19:30: "When he had received the drink, Jesus said, 'It is finished.' With that, he bowed his head and gave up his spirit."

In Christ, the work of purging is finished. We are fully accepted by God on account of what Jesus has done for us. This is the gift that keeps on giving. It's not guilt; it is grace.

Having considered the five reasons why many Evangelicals migrate from their Catholic background, we are now in a position to explore what Catholic faith actually looks like on the ground. In particular, we'll learn to communicate in ways that commend the Lord Jesus. We begin by asking the question, How do Catholics view Evangelicals?

Part 2

RELATING TO ROMAN CATHOLICS

Chapter 9

HOW CATHOLICS VIEW EVANGELICALS

> The LORD said to Job: "Will the one who contends with the Almighty correct him? Let him who accuses God answer him!" Then Job answered the LORD: "I am unworthy—how can I reply to you? I put my hand over my mouth."
>
> —Job 40:1–4

When God confronts us, it's appropriate to cover our mouths. Actually, biblical precedent also would have us fall prostrate in humility. The holy character of God deserves, indeed requires, such a response. And when *people* confront us, we might not go prostrate, but we must listen carefully nonetheless, for people are made in God's image. If it requires that we cover our mouths, so be it; whatever it takes to accurately hear what they have to say. Such attention is not only courteous; it's deeply theological.

After having thus far expressed numerous observations about the Catholic Church, it's time for me to let Catholics speak. In particular, we want to hear Catholics describe their perceptions of Evangelicals —the things we say and do that get their attention and perhaps make them want to run away. Not only must we listen carefully, we must let their critique lead us into self-evaluation and at some points even repentance. Not only do the virtues of humility and faithfulness require this of us, so does wisdom, for these insights have the power to greatly improve our communication with Catholic loved ones.

SALVATION AS "FIRE INSURANCE"

Let me offer you an example of this critique from an article published by Ms. Anna Nussbaum in 2004 when she was a junior at the University of Notre Dame. It comes from the pages of *Commonweal*, a religious journal edited and managed by lay Catholics.

> The flight to East Africa was a red-eye, but it was daytime on my body clock, and I was fatigued from several days of traveling alone. So I prayed, drank a lot of water, did stretches in the aisle, and tried not to watch the in-flight TVs broadcasting the beheading of a U.S. civilian in Iraq. Waiting in line to use the bathroom, a white man in his sixties from the United States struck up a conversation. "What's your business in Africa?" he asked cordially. "I'm going to teach English in a Holy Cross school," I replied, trying to muster the confidence I thought those words demanded. "The school's outside Jinja and I'll be working with the CSCs and the Holy Cross Associates nearby." Then I asked him what he would be doing in Uganda, and he told me that he was a Bible translator, and that he was working with an organization that translated the New Testament into African languages. I smiled. Then he asked me, "Are you saved?"
>
> "No," I said, still smiling. "I'm Catholic."
>
> His blue eyes glistened as he raised his eyebrows. "But are you a Christian? Do you believe in Jesus Christ?" he asked, growing more and more animated. I hesitated. "Yes," I said. "I believe in Jesus Christ." I was trying to be respectful.
>
> "But who do you believe that he is?" the missionary asked. It was a good question, and a difficult one to answer while waiting for the lavatory. Discomfort set in, and I wanted the man to leave me alone. He reminded me of the fundamentalists who would come to the park across the street from my

> public high school and ask those of us who looked tough if we would accept Jesus as our personal savior. I answered his question as best I could: "I believe he's the savior of the universe," and looked down at my socks. "Then why won't you get saved right now?!" he coaxed.
>
> Had I given the wrong answer?
>
> "What if this plane were to plunge into that icy water? What if this plane crashed? Are you certain that you'd go to heaven? Are you?"
>
> I looked him straight in the face and said, "No, I'm not," as my mind drifted to the churning ocean thirty-five thousand feet below. *When did I see him naked and clothe him? When did I see him hungry and give him food?*
>
> I couldn't say this at the risk of upsetting him further, and, waiting to pee, I wasn't prepared to defend a faith-and-works theology. I couldn't say a thing. I was too frustrated and on edge to speak. My missionary friend continued preaching until the lavatory door opened and I escaped inside.[1]

There are a host of insights worth teasing out of Anna's experience; however, I'd like to focus on a particular one. Why do you suppose Anna's mind drifted to Jesus' words about clothing the naked and feeding the hungry? I feel pretty confident of the answer, even though I've not had opportunity to communicate with Anna. It was a reaction to the Evangelical tendency to treat salvation like fire insurance.

On one level I applaud the effort of the Evangelical man who shared his faith. He cared enough to present the gospel, which is more than can be said for many of us. However, his approach left something to be desired. Like a charging ram relentlessly slamming into its victim, the Evangelical aggressively pressed forward undaunted by (or perhaps oblivious to) Anna's responses. In doing so, he reduced the

---

1. Anna Nussbaum, "Slowly By Slowly What Africa Taught Me," *Commonweal*, December 17, 2004. © 2004 Commonweal Foundation, reprinted with permission. For subscriptions: *www.commonwealmagazine.org*.

gospel, in her eyes at least, to "saying the prayer." This is the caricature that Catholics have of Evangelicals. Salvation is like fire insurance: simply "get saved" and you're covered.

I believe this is why Anna referred to Jesus' command to care for the needy. Far from "easy-believism" or "cheap grace," authentic Christianity defines conversion as necessarily dying to self and being set apart to serve Christ. It is our identity as the new creation for whom the old has gone and the new has come (2 Cor. 5:17). Such life is marked by "incarnational" service, embodying the love of Jesus to the world. More than private spirituality, it is a public mission with Jesus at the center inspiring his church to exhibit and extend redemption in tangible ways. Therefore, promising one salvation on the basis of a single prayer not only sounds like reductionism, it smacks of heresy. I'm inclined to give the Evangelical man on the plane the benefit of the doubt—that he would agree with our insistence on obedience. Many Evangelicals, however, stand before the accusation of cheap grace guilty as charged.

Anna and our Catholic friends are correct. The idea that one can simply articulate a sinner's prayer and solely on that basis be assured of salvation is misguided. It's certainly not what the Protestant Reformers taught. They made it clear that justification is by faith alone, but not by a faith that is alone.[2] As John Calvin stated, "For we dream neither of a faith devoid of good works nor of a justification that stands without them."[3] The same emphasis continued among subsequent Evangelicals, as Jonathan Edwards wrote: "And one great thing he [Jesus] aimed at in redemption, was to deliver them from their idols, and bring them to God."[4] From the sixteenth century to the present,

2. Or in the *Westminster Confession of Faith*: "Faith, thus receiving and resting on Christ and His righteousness, is the alone instrument of justification: yet is it not alone in the person justified, but is ever accompanied with all other saving graces, and is no dead faith, but works by love" (*Westminster Confession of Faith*, "Of Justification," chap. 11.2).

3. John Calvin, *Institutes of the Christian Religion*, 2 vols., ed. John T. McNeill, trans. Ford Lewis Battles (Louisville: Westminster John Knox, 1960), 1:798 (3.16.1).

4. Jonathan Edwards, *The Works of Jonathan Edwards*, vol. 2, "Discourse: Men Naturally Are God's Enemies" (1834; repr., Peabody, MA: Hendrickson, 1998), 139.

Evangelical theology at its best has taught that the purpose of salvation is maturity in Christ for the glory of God, not fire insurance.

More important than the writings of Evangelical Reformers is the sacred text of Scripture. The Bible puts great emphasis upon the need for obedience. As James asserts in his letter, "What good is it, my brothers, if a man claims to have faith but has no deeds? Can such faith save him? Suppose a brother or sister is without clothes and daily food. If one of you says to him, 'Go, I wish you well; keep warm and well fed,' but does nothing about his physical needs, what good is it? In the same way, faith by itself, if it is not accompanied by action, is dead" (James 2:14–17).

Another valuable example is from Ephesians. We Evangelicals often quote 2:8–9 to argue on behalf of free grace: "For it is by grace you have been saved, through faith—and this not from yourselves, it is the gift of God—not by works, so that no one can boast."

Unfortunately, we stop short of verse 10, which brings Paul's thought to completion: "For we are God's workmanship, created in Christ Jesus to do good works, which God prepared in advance for us to do."

J. I. Packer explains how this tradition ultimately is rooted in the teaching of Jesus: "A man must know that, in the words of the first of Luther's Ninety-five Theses, 'when our Lord and Master, Jesus Christ, said "Repent," He called for the entire life of believers to be one of repentance,' and he must also know what repentance involves. More than once, Christ deliberately called attention to the radical break with the past that repentance involves. 'If any man will come after me, let him *deny himself*, and take up his cross daily, and follow me ... whosoever will *lose his life for my sake*, the same (but only he) shall save it.' "[5]

Remembering our analogy of Luther's dung hill, we must be cautious. While the basis by which sinners are accepted by God is their identification with the crucified and resurrected Christ, which comes

5. J. I. Packer, *Evangelism and the Sovereignty of God* (Downers Grove, IL: InterVarsity, 1991), 72.

by grace alone (Eph. 2:8–9), the authenticity of this faith will necessarily manifest itself in godly behavior—good works (Eph. 2:10).

An old professor and friend of mine liked to explain the need for works in salvation in terms of a Costco card. Most parts of the country probably have Costco or an equivalent. It is a membership warehouse chain that offers customers discounts on a wide array of products because merchandise is purchased in bulk. The transaction that provides access to Costco occurs when one becomes a member. You simply pay the fee, get your membership card with an embarrassing photo, and shop to your heart's desire. Whenever you visit the store, you must present your card to the nice lady at the door to verify that you have paid the price of membership. This card-showing exercise, which is performed in all subsequent visits, simply confirms that you have already completed the membership transaction.[6]

So it is with good works in salvation. Our virtuous behavior can never procure or somehow enhance God's favor. The cost of forgiveness and new life is infinite and we are bankrupt. Only Christ can complete the transaction for us, which he did by shedding his blood. By dying on the cross as our substitute and rising from the dead, Jesus enabled us to approach the throne of grace with confidence. But not only do we have confidence; God also has sent his Holy Spirit to live within us and has blessed us with every spiritual blessing in heaven in order for the church to walk in good works which he prepared beforehand. Therefore, we must regard salvation to be much more than eternal life insurance that gets us into heaven. God's unmerited favor must take the form of an obedient life of faith here and now, as Paul the apostle writes: "Since we have these promises, dear friends, let us purify ourselves from everything that contaminates body and spirit, perfecting holiness out of reverence for God" (2 Cor. 7:1).

---

6. Like all analogies, there are a few points where the Costco card comparison breaks down. For example, when your membership expires, you must purchase another one. You will also perform another monetary transaction when you buy products from the store. For some reason, I find these payments are always quite large.

EXCURSUS: SOMETHING EVANGELICALS CAN LEARN FROM CATHOLICS

Evangelicals seem to have a theological illness. It's not a condition that you can easily identify like lice or athlete's foot. It's much more subtle, like a parasitic tapeworm that hides in your digestive tract for months before you discover it. Philosophers call it a platonic dualism. It's an outlook that regards spiritual things to be inherently superior to the physical world—spirit is good; matter is evil.

When Catholics identify our illness, they often do so with the following phrase: "You're so heavenly minded that you're no earthly good!" These words describe the tendency of Evangelicals to be overly spiritual on one hand and on the other oblivious to the practical needs of society. As one Evangelical preacher was fond of saying, "Don't carry a loaf of bread in one hand and the Bible in the other, lest in your efforts to feed the poor you forget that you're carrying the Word of God."

Very often we don't realize that we have the theological tapeworm until our Catholic friends reveal it to us by their positive example. What I'm referring to is the Catholic practice of positively engaging culture, what is often called social action. Following from their emphasis on the principle of incarnation, Catholic ministry is concerned with how the life of Christ addresses the tangible dimensions of our world. Whether it's education, politics, economics, sexual issues, prison reform, poverty, race issues, or sanctity of life, Catholics operate with a robust moral theology that is generally foreign to Evangelicalism.

In my role as pastor of community outreach, I am keenly aware of how much we struggle with understanding how gospel ministry relates to the enterprise of cultural engagement. In our church we have a pretty good grasp on what needs to happen in the name of evangelism, but our handle on social outreach is clumsy at best.

Thankfully, there seems to be a growing awareness among Evangelicals today of the need to repent of our unbiblical dualisms. These often-younger Evangelical leaders have somehow removed their tapeworms and therefore have an appetite to enrich culture as constructive agents of Christ's kingdom. I'll close this section with a quote from one of these agents who extricated his tapeworm long ago, if he ever had one—the British pastor John Stott: "It is exceedingly strange that any followers of Jesus Christ should ever have needed to ask whether social involvement was their concern, and that controversy should have blown up over the relationship between Evangelicalism and social responsibility. For it is evident that in his public ministry Jesus both 'went about ... teaching ... and preaching' (Matt 4.23; 9.35 RSV) and 'went about doing good and healing' (Acts 10.38 RSV). In consequence, evangelism and social concern have been intimately related to one another throughout the history of the Church."[7]

"CHUMMY CHUMMY" WITH GOD

As a child, I once made the mistake of picking up a pack of matches from the roadside. Having watched adults strike matchsticks for years, it seemed natural to give it a try. Fortunately, my father noticed my pyromania before I had gotten very far. His swift intervention left such an impression that my desire to see flames was extinguished at once.

Scripture says that our "God is a consuming fire." Apart from mercy, divine holiness would reduce humanity to a lump of charred ashes. Nonetheless, Evangelicals have a habit of behaving nonchalantly toward God, as though he were a snowflake instead of an inferno. This is why Catholics describe us as "overly chummy." For instance, Anne Dillard articulates the Catholic concern: "On the whole, I do not find Christians, outside the catacombs, sufficiently sensible of the conditions [of God's presence]. Does anyone have the foggiest idea what sort of power we so blithely invoke? Or, as I suspect, does no one believe a word of it? The churches are children playing on the floor

7. John Stott, *Issues Facing Christians Today: A Major Appraisal of Contemporary Social and Moral Questions* (Basingstoke: Marshalls, 1984), 2.

with their chemistry sets, mixing up a batch of TNT to kill a Sunday morning. It is madness to wear ladies' straw hats and velvet hats to church; we should all be wearing crash helmets. Ushers should issue life preservers and signal flares; they should lash us to our pews. For the sleeping god may wake some day and take offense; or the waking god may draw us out to where we can never return."[8]

The Catholic perspective is partly influenced by a different understanding of social order. When the Protestant Reformers reshaped the church's understanding of vocation, destroying the medieval distinction between the spiritual (that which the church controlled) and secular (social institutions and conventions outside of the church), the sacred ground was thereby leveled. One didn't have to be among the religious elite or clergy to enjoy an intimate relationship with God.

The problem with many Evangelicals, though, is that we emphasize this ground leveling to the degree that we forget the unfathomable weight of God's holiness. In the words of J. B. Phillips, "Our God is too small." When this happens, we address the Almighty as we would a mere mortal. In the face of such pride and self-sufficiency, our Catholic friends remind us of what it looks like to approach God with reverence. We may disagree with their theological or liturgical underpinnings, but their emphasis on humility and holy fear is something we must appreciate and indeed learn from.

ABSENCE OF UNITY

Ice cubes have come a long way. A century ago, cubes were delivered in one enormous block. When I was a child, my family used ice-cube trays. Today, however, if you need to fill a beverage cooler before a picnic or ball game, you needn't even touch a tray. Many refrigerators produce cubes one at a time. Simply position your cooler below the dispenser, push the button, and watch individual pieces of ice roll out of the door.

As the ice cube has gone, so has the Evangelical church. This is true at least in Western culture, where one's identity is no longer

8. Annie Dillard, *Teaching a Stone to Talk* (New York: Harper and Row, 1982), 40–41.

defined by the block (the Catholic Church) or the tray (a denomination in which there's a shared ecclesial structure). Instead, Evangelicals are individuals who roll out the door with little-to-no commitment to church membership.

Given the depth of individualism within most Evangelical circles, Catholics often see us as a multitude of isolated believers bereft of unity. We have no papal leader, no bishops to govern, no common liturgy to stabilize public worship, and a lack of agreement about what constitutes orthodox belief and practice. What we do have are a million different senior pastors who seem to make decisions based on the whims of their preferences. Evangelicals see this fragmentation as "unfortunate"; for Catholics, however, it's a travesty which undermines Evangelical legitimacy.

One component of the problem is Catholics' lack of familiarity with Protestantism. When the typical symbols of religion are absent (liturgy, clerics, and statuary), Catholics assume an absence of religious life. Also, because Protestant denominations are distinct institutions, Catholics who view the church institutionally naturally overlook the fundamental unity shared by these denominations—unity around basic doctrinal propositions; that is, "the gospel."

It is a very rare Catholic indeed who is conversant with the historical events between Martin Luther and a modern figure like Billy Graham. And why should they be? If you belong to the one, holy, catholic, and apostolic church, there's really no need for you to consider the ecclesial alternatives. To put it crassly, if you own a set of Big Bertha golf clubs, there's no point in concerning yourself with the imitation knockoffs.

Perhaps the fundamental reason why Catholics and Evangelicals have such a radically different perspective on the necessity of unity is the doctrine that we addressed earlier, called continuous incarnation. Catholics who maintain this view understand the life of Jesus to extend into the world in and through the tangible structures of the Roman Catholic Church. Without this institutional solidarity, there is no longer a unified church, so the logic goes.

In responding to the critique of individualism, we should recognize that Catholics have once again put their finger on a legitimate flaw within Evangelicalism. On the whole, we suffer from an anemic ecclesiology, which is to say that we don't appreciate the necessity of Christian unity. Pastor Josh Moody explains how we are guilty of this error: "We, in conservative Christian circles, have vigorously maintained the *message* of the gospel but, at least in some areas and among some movements, have begun to lose any profound grasp of the community of Christ. We have rightly said that a relationship with God is a personal matter. In our context, though, it has become but a step, and a step many of us have unthinkingly taken, to acquiesce that a relationship with God is a purely *individual* matter. This is practical heterodoxy. Jesus said you can identify his disciples by the kind of relationship they have with *one another*, by the love they have for one another."[9]

In the same vein as Moody, New Testament theologian Robert Banks presses on this problem when he writes, "Paul's understanding of community is nothing less than the gospel in corporate form!"[10] Think about that for a moment.

When a careful scholar like Banks makes such a bold and provocative statement, we should pay close attention. In a simple sentence he hits us between the eyes with an aspect of salvation that often eludes us: when God redeems us, he births us into his community. Each of us represents a living stone which God enjoins to form a spiritual house (Eph. 2:19–22; 1 Peter 2:4–10). We are members of Christ's body, organically connected to one another (Rom. 12:3–8; 1 Cor. 12:12–31). The Lord Jesus himself prays for this unity, asking the Father to make us one, just as the triune God is one (John 17:11), and the apostle Paul exhorts us to earnestly preserve our oneness (Eph. 4:3). Anything less is sub-Christian.

---

9. Josh Moody, *The God-Centered Life: Insights from Jonathan Edwards for Today* (Vancouver: Regent College Publishing, 2006), 113.
10. Robert Banks, *Paul's Idea of Community* (Peabody, MA: Hendrickson, 1994), 190.

SUPERFICIALITY

In his book *Holyland USA*, Peter Feuerherd, a Catholic journalist, describes what he observed in America's largest Evangelical theme park. He writes,

> I was surrounded by shorts and T-shirts proclaiming The Rock, The Lamb — even one that says Read Between the Lines, with a picture of the back of a crucified Christ, complete with stark red blood stripes. When we enter, the sign for the cafeteria advertises Goliath Burgers and Bedouin beef.[11]
>
> My wife and friends wonder if I have a screw loose. No self-respecting liberal-thinking northeasterner would venture into such a strange world, a place where the worldviews of Disney and Jimmy Swaggart intersect. The 10-year-old daughter of a Catholic friend of mine sees it as sacrilegious to combine the sacred and the profane in a Holy Land amusement park.[12]

I want to pick up on the ten-year-old girl's comment. Why would the Holy Land Theme Park have Evangelical ten-year-old girls eating Goliath Burgers with sheer delight while their Catholic counterparts are offended by the idea? The former regards the sword of the Spirit letter opener and widow's mite pendant, which she purchased in the gift shop, to be positive contributions to society, or at least to her own life. The latter regards such trinkets as religious compromise and wholesale capitulation to popular culture, even if she doesn't say it in those words.

Toward the end of his book, Feuerhard speaks to this question when he writes, "Evangelicals are pioneers in bringing American pop culture and baptizing it into the Christian realm."[13] He might be right. When this cultural baptism is done responsibly, we call it con-

---

11. Peter Feuerherd, *Holyland USA: A Catholic Ride through America's Evangelical Landscape* (New York: Crossroad, 2006), 2.
12. Ibid., 151–52.
13. Ibid., 160.

textualization, meaning that we've sought to translate biblical truth to our modern context. Catholics and Evangelicals ordinarily agree that this activity is good and necessary. As Paul the apostle expressed it, "I have become all things to all men so that by all possible means I might save some" (1 Cor. 9:22). However, when it's done poorly, we call it something like the trivialization of God, the Evangelical subculture's shallow side, or cheesy merchandizing. Unfortunately, Evangelicals are famous for leaning in the latter direction.

When you speak with Catholics about popular Evangelical culture, you find they have a mixture of amusement, bewilderment, and repulsion. Given the place of tradition, reverence, and austerity in Catholic liturgy, it's not surprising. When sacred value is assigned to tangible items like statues, stained glass, and holy water fonts, the absence of all such concrete symbols naturally leads Catholics to conclude that sacredness is likewise absent. Simply contrast the rich complexity and texture of most Catholic parishes with the minimalist style of Evangelical churches, particularly in some megachurches where you're unlikely to find even a simple cross, and you can better understand why Evangelical culture leaves many Catholics feeling uncomfortable.

Part of this Catholic critique is influenced by a difficulty appreciating the extent of Jesus' humanity, a common Catholic tendency. Let me explain how this gets worked out.

The following story is told of G. K. Chesterton (1874–1936), an eminent British author from a previous generation: "One day the great British writer G. K. Chesterton was barreling down a street in London, preoccupied with weighty thoughts, his thick cape flying behind him. As he turned a corner, head down, he collided with a man rolling a grandfather clock down the narrow sidewalk. Chesterton brushed himself off, scowled at the man, and shouted, 'Why can't you just wear a wristwatch like everyone else?' "[14]

---

14. Ellen Vaughn, *Time Peace: Living Here and Now with a Timeless God* (Grand Rapids, MI: Zondervan, 2007), 61.

Chesterton was not only brilliant; he was brilliantly funny. However, while a sharp wit was one of his shining qualities, it's fascinating to read what he had to say about the humor of Jesus. At the conclusion of his classic book *Orthodoxy* he writes, "There was one thing that was too great for God to show us when He walked upon our earth; and I have sometimes fancied that it was His mirth."[15]

We don't use the word *mirth* very much today. It describes gladness expressed through hearty laughter. Chesterton was saying that he couldn't imagine the incarnated Jesus laughing out loud. The austere God-man walked in real sandals, ate real food, drank real wine, but he never went so far as to laugh. Far be it from me, an insignificant first-time author, to take issue with a literary titan like Chesterton; however, in this instance I must humbly disagree.

I'd like to suggest that Chesterton's view of Jesus is representative of many Catholics. This is reflected, for example, in the Catholic girl's aversion to Goliath Burgers. She protested the sacrilegious combination of the sacred and the profane. But where do these categories come from? I'll grant that Bedouin beef is patently corny, but where do we find the notion that in Christ's new creation there are two separate spheres called sacred and profane? We must acknowledge that there is a clear difference between holiness and sin, but to categorically consign experiences like laughter and amusement to the realm of profanity is biblically unwarranted. In fact, it's worse. It leaves you with a Jesus whose feet hover six inches above his sandals but never quite touch down.

If the Catholic flaw is a less than human Christ, Evangelicals struggle with the other extreme. We conceive of Jesus in running shoes sporting a Sergio Tacchini sweatsuit and jogging beside us on the treadmill. Few of us would articulate such a crass perception, but if you listen to Evangelicals refer to God in prayer or conversation, you start to wonder. Divine imminence and personal presence are so drastically emphasized that superficiality reigns instead of the King

15. G. K. Chesterton, *Orthodoxy* (San Francisco: Ignatius, 1908), 167–68.

of Kings and Lord of Lords. One need not be a biblical theologian to recognize that such a view of Christ is absurd, and that where guilty of it, we Evangelicals ought to repent.

CONCLUSION

As we close this section, I must make what is perhaps the most important point. When we speak with family and friends about matters of faith, we must realize that there are a host of personal issues in the background that have just as much import for our discussions as the words themselves. Beyond the various issues that we've covered in this chapter, there are also intense hurts and fears. Let me explain.

During my research I called Martha, a distant relative on my wife's side of the family. Now in her midseventies, she remains deeply committed to her Catholic faith even though all of her five children have left the Catholic Church. I inquired into how this makes her feel, particularly in regard to the two children who are now committed Evangelical Protestants. Her response was poignant. After a pause, she responded with a simple statement: "I feel like a failure."

As I continued to talk with Martha, she explained her reason for feeling so. She and her husband had brought their children to Mass each week, sent them to parochial school, and made numerous sacrifices along the way to encourage their religious formation. However, when the kids became adults, they stopped going to Mass. Worse still, two of them became the sort of Evangelicals who held the Catholic Church in contempt and felt free to say so. From that point forward, Martha's relationship with her Evangelical children was disastrous.

It became obvious to me after listening to Martha that when it comes to talking to our Catholic families, we must realize that there are complex personal issues at play. Whether it's unfulfilled hopes and dreams, guilt, or feelings of betrayal, our loved ones have real pain. Therefore, we must be sensitive and wise whenever we engage in conversation.

Following is an example of the sort of humble sensitivity that relationships with Catholics require of us. It is written by Mark Christensen, a former Catholic who is now an Evangelical:

> I was drawn by the unobscured centrality of Christ, constantly kept in the fore through the preaching of the Gospel. Dearly loved family and friends, that is why I left and why I think most leave the Catholic Church for Evangelicalism. We didn't leave to offend you or suggest we were better than you. We didn't leave to say that we didn't want that part of your past or that you had done anything wrong in raising us. We left because we met Jesus Christ, and He changed our lives in a way that we never knew in the Catholic Church. I left because someone shared with me the same Gospel that gripped St. Peter and the apostles and martyrs and thousands of Catholic and Protestants saints since. I came to understand who Jesus is and why He came to earth.[16]

Our opportunity is to express this idea with grace and truth. May God help us!

The next chapter is critical. If we are to have a chance at relating to our Catholic loved ones, we must understand them. We will seek to do this by analyzing the three most prominent types of Catholics in America today.

---

16. Mark Christensen, "Coming to Grips with Losses: The Migration of Catholics into Conservative Protestantism," *America*, 26 January 1991, 58–59.

Chapter 10

TRADITIONAL, EVANGELICAL, AND CULTURAL CATHOLICS

My grandfather's nose had been broken on a few occasions, and it showed. At one point during childhood I mustered up enough courage to ask why his nose wasn't exactly centered on his face. He described an occasion when he stepped in between two brawling friends and suddenly caught a flying fist.

What I'm attempting to do in this chapter is about as safe as stepping into a brawl. Given limitations of space, it's bound to feel like some people I describe are being misrepresented. Let me say up front: I apologize. As I mentioned earlier, it's the liability of developing profiles. But we need profiles; otherwise, we'll continue to misunderstand our Catholic friends. Given the choice, I suppose I'd rather get poked with a punch than sheepishly sit on the sidelines afraid to enter the fray. Each profile is a thumbnail sketch which invites finer distinction. Nevertheless, of the primary sources of authority on which Catholic faith is based, tradition, the Bible, and culture are the big three. From these foundational commitments, religious identity grows into shape.

At this point one might properly ask what the goal is of this communication that I'm proposing. Am I suggesting that we target every single Catholic person for proselytism, and if so, what am I assuming about the legitimacy of their Christian faith? Let me offer an answer so you know where I'm coming from.

Only God knows for sure the state of someone's soul. It says in 1 Samuel 16:7, "Man looks at the outward appearance, but the LORD looks at the heart." Being well acquainted with the deception in my own heart, I'm reticent to pronounce whether a Christ-follower who fears God is a genuine believer. Who of us knows for sure? I expect that we'll all be somewhat surprised when we hear the roll call in heaven and find out who is present (assuming, of course, that we ourselves persevere to the end).

Thankfully, the Holy Spirit produces virtuous fruit in the life of a believer to indicate that we are indeed his children. Such fruit should be celebrated for the glory of God and looked to as verification that we are truly in the faith (2 Cor. 13:5). However, we must be careful about appointing ourselves fruit inspectors who dogmatically assert who is in and who is outside of Christ.

So what's the purpose of communicating with Catholics about the gospel? I would contend that it's the same purpose that drives gospel communication between Evangelicals, or for that matter, it's the reason why I must preach to myself every single day. Because the gospel is bigger than the moment of one's conversion, reaching forward to define and transform all of life, we must constantly remind one another that Jesus Christ is Lord (2 Cor. 10:3–5; Col. 3:16). It's the enterprise of encouraging and exhorting ourselves to hate sin and love Jesus, as it says in Hebrews 3:12–13: "See to it, brothers, that none of you has a sinful, unbelieving heart that turns away from the living God. But encourage one another daily, as long as it is called 'Today,' so that none of you may be hardened by sin's deceitfulness." Thus, sharing the hope of Jesus with a Catholic friend or family member doesn't presume to judge his or her spiritual state. Rather, it highlights the dire importance of proclaiming Christ's redemption to the world.

THE TRADITIONAL CATHOLIC

I'd like to start with a quote from *Holyland USA* by Catholic author Peter Feuerherd. We must understand his observation concerning the varied and complex shape of Catholicism: "In reality, Catholicism includes those with disparate authority and opinions about almost everything under the sun. There are liberal bishops and conservative bishops. The pope sometimes differs with his own Curia. American Catholic voters are regularly viewed by experts as a crucial swing group in every national election, too diffuse to truly categorize. In fact, some scholars of religion refer to Catholicism as the Hinduism of Christianity, because it is infused with so many different schools of prayer, ritual and perspective, much like the native and diverse religions of India now referred to under the single rubric of Hinduism."[1]

Feuerherd's point is helpful to keep in mind. It's easy to see the common clerical attire of priests, the standard liturgical order of the Mass, and the hierarchical structure that unifies parishes and conclude that there is general unity in the Catholic Church. Not quite. Just like in Protestantism, there are progressives and conservatives, charismatics and stoics, feminists and male elitists, postmodern relativists, liberation theologians, traditionalists, mystics, and everything in between.

Of the various types of Catholics just mentioned, the traditional Catholic is probably closest to what we would call the fundamentalist. People of this mind understand the basic authority of Christian faith to be the teaching of the church, with the pope as its chief spokesman. It is, if you will, the Vatican I mindset. Proponents generally manifest the following characteristics:

- Have a high regard for Catholic clergy
- Regard faith as private
- Rarely practice personal Bible reading

1. Peter Feuerherd, *Holyland USA: A Catholic Ride through America's Evangelical Landscape* (New York: Crossroad, 2006), 72.

- View Protestants as heretics or sub-Christian
- Some attend a Latin Mass (though most don't)
- Regard the phrase "personal relationship with Jesus" as presumptuous

Two years ago I considered this group to be small and mainly elderly, but after listening to Catholic radio and communicating with various Catholics, I think this position is probably more prominent that many of us realize. Let me give you an example.

At the start of my research I decided to contact two Catholic apologists (individuals who explain the Catholic faith to nonbelievers) to develop friendships with them. I had two purposes in mind: (1) for them to hold me accountable to fair and accurate writing, and, (2) to practice what I'm proposing in this book, which is to relate to Catholics with grace and truth. They both eventually responded to my emails. The first one expressed discomfort talking to someone like me who has considered the evidence for Catholic faith and rejected it. The second was disinterested, although he did offer to debate me on the doctrine of Scripture alone. Since I'm not citing their names, I'll give you an example right out of my email inbox. In response to an announcement telling friends that this book had been picked up by Zondervan, one of them responded with one sentence, "I will be happy to write a rebuttal to the book if in fact it is against the Catholic and apostolic faith."

I know what you're thinking. Surely not every traditional Catholic is so disagreeable. I'm sure you're right. What I want to emphasize, though, is traditional Catholics' attitude toward Evangelicals. Simply put, Evangelicals constitute an illegitimate, potentially threatening form of Christianity. When we talk to these people about the gospel, we appear to them as wolves in sheep's clothing, instruments of the Evil One who try to undermine the work of Christ.

Before we're too hard on traditional Catholics, we must realize that from their perspective they're simply being faithful. Think of it this way. How do you feel when a Mormon or a Jehovah's Witness visits your little sister, son, or granddaughter with an invitation to visit their kingdom hall? Because Evangelicals view these groups as cults outside the pale of Christian orthodoxy, we feel defensive and, if we're honest, less than loving toward those who attempt to undermine the faith. This is the sort of obstacle we're dealing with when we talk to a traditional Catholic.

When communicating with traditional Catholics we must be conscious of their particular values and then approach them accordingly. Following is a short list of the ones we need to be aware of:

- We must not take cheap shots at the Catholic clergy.
- Because traditional Catholics consider faith to be a private matter, we must broach the subject of spiritual things slowly and carefully. Imagine you're driving through rural Illinois with a traditional Catholic, and you comment on the cows eating grass. "Look at the strong legs of that bull, all four of them, wow! By the way, have you heard of the four spiritual laws ..." Few of us would take so crass an approach (I trust), but I share it to underscore the principle. Instead of questions that seem to come out of the blue, we need to *gradually* direct attention to the things of God.
- We need to use Scripture when talking with traditional Catholics because God's Word is the appointed means by which individuals encounter Christ, but when we enter a room wielding the Bible like Bruce Lee or Jackie Chan swinging a pair of nunchucks, we're unlikely to administer the Word of life very effectively. We must share Scripture in a spirit of love.
- Since traditional Catholics view Evangelicals as heterodox (those who have incorrect and unacceptable teaching), we must concentrate on establishing credibility and rapport with traditional Catholics. They must know that we sincerely care for them and don't view them as potential notches in the handles of our evangelistic pistols.

- I don't know what to say to people who insist the Latin Mass. I'm tempted to ask them why Latin is so important to them when the Bible was written in Hebrew, Aramaic, and Greek, but taking this approach undermines the principle I'm trying to promote. If Latin comes up, change the subject.
- Because traditional Catholics emphasize the transcendence of God (that God is exalted over creation), the phrase "personal relationship with Jesus" sounds presumptuous. As a Catholic friend once said to me, "When Evangelicals pray, they sound like they're talking to a golf buddy instead of almighty God." He's right. God is indeed transcendent and deserves our reverence. This is something we can affirm about the Catholic tradition. At the same time, we have the opportunity to point out that God draws near in the person of his Son. This immanent presence of God is especially helpful to convey when someone experiences suffering. Biblical passages dealing with the closeness of God are just what hurting hearts need on such occasions.

THE EVANGELICAL CATHOLIC

In his book *Evangelical Catholics?* author Keith Fournier asks a provocative question: Can a Catholic also be Evangelical? To many people this sounds like a contradiction in terms. "Take your pick," they retort, "Catholic or Evangelical, but you can't have both." According to Fournier, however, the answer is yes! Speaking as a lay Catholic, Fournier insists that to be truly Catholic means that one is simultaneously Evangelical.[2] In his own words: "The challenge I have as a Catholic Christian is the same as it is for any [Evangelical] Christian: to bring people to Jesus Christ, to a personal decision to accept Him as Savior and Lord, to bring them to personal repentance and conver-

2. Keith Fournier, *Evangelical Catholics?* (Nashville: Thomas Nelson, 1990), 21–23. This widely used category of "Evangelical Catholic" remains problematic in that it often doesn't include a commitment to the doctrine of justification by faith alone, which is central to Evangelical belief and identity. Nevertheless, the term continues to be used in a sociological sense by Catholics and Protestants alike.

sion.... The Church exists to evangelize, a mission entrusted to her by her Head, Master, and Lord, the Evangel Himself, Jesus Christ."[3]

If you're familiar with the legacy of Vatican II, you understand where the emphasis on personal faith and evangelism comes from. The other influential force behind Evangelical Catholicism is the charismatic movement which flourished in the 1970s and continues to be a vibrant impulse today. Very often Catholic charismatic parishes are virtually indistinguishable from their Protestant counterparts (notwithstanding the Mass), as the following description illustrates: "A charismatic style of prayer is common at Christ the King [Catholic Church]. People are free to raise their hands in prayer and during songs, many pray their own prayers audibly, some pray in tongues, etc.... They pray with expressive or charismatic prayer at monthly parish prayer meetings, at the beginning of parish meetings, and most especially during certain moments in the Holy Mass. These are some of the external markers of a charismatic parish. Internal markers include a radical surrender to the Lordship of Jesus Christ in all parts of life, a strong adherence to the Gospel and the teachings of the Catholic Church, and the pursuit of strong friendships centered on Christ."[4]

Charismatic or not, Evangelical Catholics possess a faith that is personal, Jesus centered, and outreach oriented. These qualities constitute the bridge which connects them to Evangelical Protestants. Take, for instance, the outreach program called Alpha. Born at Holy Trinity Church Brompton, an Anglican church in London, England, Alpha is an evangelistic ministry that welcomes nonchurched visitors to several consecutive weeks of dinner, explanation of the Christian message, and discussion. For two decades the program has gained enormous popularity in many Protestant denominations, and is now being used in Catholic parishes, with official support from bishops and priests.[5]

---

3. Ibid. 18–19.
4. *www.rc.net/lansing/ctk*.
5. Notably by Cardinal Christoph Schonborn, Archbishop of Vienna; and Cardinal Walter Kasper, president of the Pontifical Council for Promoting Christian Unity.

Distinctive Catholic teaching is usually added as a supplement, but otherwise, the message of personal faith in Jesus remains the same.

Some parts of the country have a higher concentration of Evangelical Catholics.[6] Generally, you'll find more in communities where there's a preponderance of Evangelical Protestant churches.[7] For instance, I can think of only two Evangelical Catholics on Long Island. On the other hand, most Catholics that I meet in Wheaton, Illinois, are of the Evangelical variety. You'll know you're talking to an Evangelical Catholic when you observe the following qualities:

- Less likely to regard faith as a private matter
- Practices personal Bible reading
- Views Protestants as brothers and sisters
- May be charismatic
- A personal relationship with Jesus is a chief value

Recently, I spent a Saturday with some Evangelical Catholics. The night before, I received a voice mail message from a church member named Chad. My buddy Chad works in an office with a sizable balance of Catholics and Evangelicals. Supposedly, when other stockbrokers talk cigars and wine cellars, he and his Catholic colleagues debate theology.

Chad called to tell me that the famed Catholic apologist Scott Hahn was coming to the area and that one of Chad's stockbroker colleagues, named Chris, had an extra ticket. Knowing about my research, he invited me to attend in his place. Within minutes Chris and I established a rendezvous spot at St. Mary of the Annunciation Church for the next morning.

Part of Hahn's popularity comes from his personal story. He had been an Evangelical before converting to Catholicism. I knew about

---

6. According to the American Religious Identification Survey of 2008, 18.4 percent of Catholics identify themselves as "born again" (Barry A. Kosmin and Ariela Keysar, *ARIS: Summary Report*, March 2009 [Hartford: Trinity College]).

7. For more on this trend, see the article by John L. Allen Jr., "The Triumph of Evangelical Catholicism," *National Catholic Reporter*, 31 August 2007, 5–7.

him because he attended Gordon-Conwell Seminary several years before me and was an outstanding student there. With my laptop battery fully charged, I drove to Mundelein expecting to learn.

The church sanctuary was filled to capacity—more than seven hundred people. It was much like a Bible conference, except for the statues and holy water. As Scott spoke, I surveyed the crowd and made some interesting observations. Many people had Bibles in their laps, something I had never seen among Catholics on the East Coast. During breaks, they discussed faith in personal terms. They purchased books, CDs, and talked about how to share the gospel with nonbelievers.

Chris, my host, took me and his friends to a restaurant for lunch, where we enjoyed an interchange about our religious differences and similarities. Halfway through the grilled salmon and rice pilaf, the light went on. These folks were the Evangelical Catholics about whom Fournier wrote. They felt free to talk about their personal relationship with Jesus, and in the same breath they affirmed the real presence of Christ in the Eucharist. From their perspective they possessed the fullness of Evangelical faith, unlike me with my anemic ecclesiology.

Chris was determined for us to have dinner with Scott Hahn. Kind of like Jesus when he walked through the dense crowd of offended Jews who tried to throw him off the cliff, Chris managed to weave through the enormous throng surrounding Hahn to deliver an invitation. Unfortunately, Scott had a plane to catch immediately after his last lecture. Undeterred, Chris offered for me to take Scott to the airport. For some reason Scott agreed.

During the forty minutes of waiting for Scott to finish signing books, I went to a nearby coffee shop and called my wife to inform her that I would arrive home late. My wife also knew about Scott's reputation through our seminary neighbor, who was his brother-in-law. Like a Jedi Knight who magically waves his fingers in a mind trick to persuade his conversation partner of his beliefs, Scott had singlehandedly influenced more Protestant conversions to Catholicism than the late Archbishop Fulton Sheen. I promised my wife that if I noticed any hypnotic finger movements I would close my eyes or jump out of the car if necessary. She was comforted.

In the hour it took to drive to O'Hare Airport, Scott and I discussed a wide range of issues. A member of the parish actually drove so that I could concentrate on talking. (We Italians must use our hands when we speak.) We talked so fast and used so many theological terms that the dear brother behind the wheel looked at us like we were speaking Japanese. We discussed Adam Christology in the Qumran community, the influence of Aquinas on Martin Luther's worldview, the importance of understanding monergism in Pauline theology, and a host of other topics. Once or twice Scott tried his Jedi apologetic, but I looked out the window before his hypnotic mojo kicked in. We disagreed seriously on a lot of things; however, we could still speak with mutual respect. This was quite different from my experience with the traditional Catholic apologists I described earlier. When I arrived home that night, I wrote down the chief lessons I had learned about relating to Evangelical Catholics:

- Because they are less likely to treat faith as a private matter, it is easier to raise questions that pertain to God. Since the enterprise of sharing Christ is a central part of their identity, it's natural to broach the subject. If you don't bring it up, they might very well discuss the gospel with you. If so, you could find yourself on the receiving end of evangelism. In such a situation, it's critical that you don't shut them down with a quick response or refutation. This is a time to listen with courtesy and to learn. Take note of what you agree upon. Affirm what is true. If you hear a statement that sounds like it's foreign to Scripture, don't necessarily jump on it with correction. Use wisdom and pray that in time you'll have the opportunity to address the topic in keeping with 1 Peter 3:15–16: "[answering] with gentleness and respect, keeping a clear conscience."
- Our common commitment to the Bible provides great opportunities for conversation with Evangelical Catholics. Many in

our Wheaton community have Bible studies in their homes or in our church building among Catholic friends. I like to say that the most fruitful form of local outreach we have at College Church is our weekly women's Bible study, in which dozens of Catholic ladies, who sometimes have minimal exposure to Bible study in their local parish, come and are spiritually fed. It all starts with a simple invitation to look into the Bible.

- Since Evangelical Catholics view Protestants as brothers and sisters, there's less of any "us versus them" barrier. Generally, there's a more positive disposition at the outset of conversation, which allows for easier progress in relationship building.
- For those of you who are charismatic Protestants, you'll be amazed by how similar your style of worship is to charismatic Catholics. I initially came to personal faith in a Pentecostal church. Shortly afterward I represented our fundraising firm at a charismatic Catholic parish in Port Saint Lucy, Florida. At an evening dessert function, I talked with parishioners about their spiritual routines and was amazed by how they resembled Pentecostalism. These folks had read many of the same books, used similar language, and pursued the same end of devotional intimacy with Christ.
- Because a personal relationship wirh Jesus is a chief value of Evangelical Catholics, it constitutes another important commonality. Much like Bible reading, we can naturally engage our friends in this area by addressing the topics of spiritual dynamics, the discipline of prayer, worship, mentoring, discipleship, service, and social justice, to name just a few.

THE CULTURAL CATHOLIC

A couple of years into my tenure at College Church I was invited to speak to medical students at a Catholic teaching hospital in Chicago. They asked me to spend thirty-five minutes answering the question, What is an Evangelical and what implications does our theology have for health care? Fifteen minutes were reserved at the end for discussion.

Rumor had it that virtually every cleric under the sun had appeared to speak in preceding months to the same question—that is, every one except for a conservative Protestant. Eventually, Evangelical students expressed their frustration to the administration about the oversight and asked that one of their own be invited. The leading voice among these students belonged to our church. Because of his persistence, I was invited.

Upon entering the classroom, I realized that medical school classes are larger than the classes I had at seminary. When I reached the lectern and looked out upon the sixty or so students, I decided to do something that Protestant preachers occasionally do. I scrapped my introduction and improvised. It went something like this: "I want to say thanks. My wife and I are deeply indebted to medical doctors. From our perspective, you are a reflection of the Divine Physician. Ever since our eldest son was diagnosed with severe hemophilia, we have seen the wonderful ways in which God uses doctors to impart life and hope to those who suffer."

After a few minutes of candid disclosure, something special happened. A deep quiet spread across the room. When I explained the challenge of accessing my son's tiny veins with a needle for his infusions, students listened with great interest. I later learned that earlier in the week the class had studied blood disorders.

The lecture went better than I could have imagined. Nods of agreement punctuated each section, with an overall sense of approval and appreciation in students' faces—that is, until we reached the question-and-answer segment. That's when the tone changed.

The turning point was a question about whether I considered Jesus to be the only way to salvation. When I answered in the affirmative, some students were visibly unhappy. Eventually, the conversation came down to a single controversial question: Is it appropriate for doctors to proactively share their faith with patients? In response, the Catholic chaplain quickly stood and interjected that under no circumstances should physicians attempt to proselytize their patients, for to do so would unfairly exploit their patients' vulnerability. With the conclusion of her statement, all eyes turned to me to hear what the Evangelical pastor would say.

After a deep breath and one of those "Help Lord" prayers, I asked the class for clarification on how the school defines holistic care; in other words, was their approach concerned with nurture of the spirit along with the body? With a positive response, I then asked the class to describe what spiritual care looks like from a Christian point of view. Piecing together answers I concluded that the gospel — the good news of Jesus' death and resurrection — is the source of spiritual healing and life. Finally, I suggested that to the extent that our hearts embrace this reality, sincerely regarding Jesus as the only remedy for spiritual death, doctors have no choice but to sensitively and lovingly share him with their patients. To do otherwise is to contradict one's calling as a holistic caregiver.

When class was dismissed, the chaplain offered to buy me lunch. Even though our views differed sharply, she was an exceedingly gracious hostess. Over chicken stir-fry we talked further about her understanding of Jesus. Her comments were along these lines: "Chris, you speak as though truth applies to people the same way. If we're honest, don't we have to admit that we all construct truth to suit our individual needs and preferences? Frankly, it makes me uncomfortable when people assert their beliefs in an absolute sort of way. Usually, these people are pushing a personal agenda. Don't get me wrong; I think it's important to have faith. The problem is when we insist that others believe just as we do. It's fine that you and other Evangelicals look to Jesus as your Savior; it's just not right to impose your view on everyone else."

Driving home, I thought about the chaplain's comments. It was evident that her view of Jesus had been influenced more than a little by postmodern thought. Accordingly, truth is subjectively constructed and relative to one's specific needs or desires. An understanding of God may be true for me without having to be true for you. It's the philosophy that undergirds the oft quoted statement, "I'm so glad your religion works for you, but please don't suggest that I need it too" (even though our claims about God are contradictory). The notion of divine truth that is authoritatively binding on all people is not only denied, it is viewed with suspicion or even contempt.

I drove home from the medical school with a mental list of how cultural Catholics compare with the other profiles:

- Typically regard faith as private
- Hold personal beliefs to be more significant than biblical or magisterial revelation
- Generally view Evangelicals as narrow, opinionated, and too exclusive
- Identification with Catholicism may be little more than a function of one's ethnic or familial heritage
- See truth as relative to one's individual needs and preferences

Perhaps you're scratching your head in confusion over why I would put the chaplain in the category of cultural Catholic. You're thinking, "The dear girl has given her life to ministry. Presumably her commitment to God rises above the water line of mere culture. In fact, her devotion might very well outpace yours, Chris."

This is a good point and an important qualifier for understanding how we're defining the profile of cultural Catholic. As for the chaplain's commitment to ministry, I have no doubt that it is firm and true. As with all of the profiles, our goal is not to judge one's heart but to recognize the sources of authority on which faith is based. The chaplain was neither traditional nor Evangelical because the sources of authority undergirding these positions—tradition and the Bible—were secondary to her subjective opinion of what constitutes religious truth. It was her personal experience of God that formed her authority. The Bible and tradition were part of the picture, but not particularly large parts.

It's probably true that when most of us think of a cultural Catholic, we think of someone who is nominal (Catholic in name). This described me for several years. When such people enter the hospital or complete a census, they register themselves as Roman Catholic, despite the fact that they've missed Mass for nine straight years. Or maybe they attend Mass twice a year, on Christmas and Easter. They are the "cafeteria Catholics" who pick and choose elements of religion to suit their taste, like a vegetarian picking lettuce and onions from the buffet line at Bubba's Rib Fest. Perhaps they go to church when they need something from God. Just like the nominal Protestant, these Catholics use the religious label even though Christianity has little or no influence upon their lives.

In northern Italy, under the portico on Via Cavazzoni, I met Rosa. Because her cafe was across the street from my residence, I visited quite often. Customers enter for their tray of *paste* (pastries), which are wrapped in decorative paper. She greets all her customers by name.

Given Rosa's outgoing personality, it was easy to discuss God with her, especially when I learned that she and her husband hail from Catania, Sicily, where I also have relatives. In much of southern Italy, there's a social Catholicism which is well acquainted with cathedrals, rosaries, and festivals. Rosa described these customs at some length.

At Italian coffee bars, you don't sit. You stand at the counter to sip your espresso, with a shot glass of carbonated water. (And by the way, cappuccino is strictly a morning drink not to be ordered after 11:00 a.m. Don't embarrass yourself as I did.) The pastries in the display case cause your mouth to water. The color and arrangement of cannoli, cornetti (cream-filled spiral pastry), and Napoletani rival the artistic quality of the Sistine Chapel. Before biting into something I couldn't quite pronounce, I asked Rosa about her relationship with Jesus. Her answer was fascinating. "My spiritual beliefs are private," she said. "The Bible I don't believe because it was written by men." She also had some rather pointed words for the Catholic clergy. Finally, and for most of her answer, she described a certain Sicilian parade dedicated to the patron saint of fishing.

I suspect that if some of my born-and-bred Evangelical congregants from Wheaton were present, they would have been flabbergasted by the extent to which Rosa's answer had nothing to do with Jesus. I, however, was not fazed in the least because twenty years ago

I would have answered much the same way. Whether it is New Age spirituality, postmodern relativism, agnostic reticence, or plain old paganism, cultural Catholics take their cues from something other than Christian teaching. In light of this tendency, the following are some suggestions for how you might communicate with your friends and loved ones who exhibit these qualities.

- Cultural Catholics regard faith to be private because they think doctrinal beliefs are largely irrelevant. Even though the pope would never endorse putting faith in the private category (read Pope Benedict's fine book titled *Truth and Tolerance* if you doubt this), doing so allows cultural Catholics to hold non-Christian views without having to give account for them. If you reach into this private realm without your friends' giving you permission, you run the risk of damaging the relationship. Therefore, as with the traditional Catholic, tread carefully when you encounter this response.
- Because personal beliefs are more significant than biblical or magisterial revelation, you are singing from a different sheet of music. Once again, such a difference doesn't mean that we jettison Scripture. Faith comes by hearing the Word of God (Rom. 10:17). However, we shouldn't expect that our cultural Catholic friends will immediately be persuaded by an idea simply because it is taught in the Bible. Here is where the power of personal testimony is helpful. Explain how God has confirmed and developed the gospel in your life. These anecdotes have enormous potential to communicate biblical truth in a way that resonates with experience-oriented minds.
- When you understand the cultural Catholic mindset toward truth—the idea that it is socially constructed and relative to one's own preferences—you can see why Evangelicals are viewed as narrow, opinionated, and overly exclusive. If my philosophy professor were speaking to this, he'd describe the situation as a "difference of epistemology." Bible-believing

Christians see truth as something that we can actually know (albeit imperfectly). It is authoritative and binding on all humanity because it proceeds from God. Our challenge is to maintain this conviction concerning the absolute nature of God's Word in a manner that is full of humility and grace, even as it says in 1 Timothy 1:5, "But the goal of our instruction is love from a pure heart and a good conscience and a sincere faith" (NASB).

- Rosa is a good example of how Catholicism can be a function of one's ethnic or familial heritage. Whether it's Polish, Irish, Italian, Filipino, Mexican, or something else, allegiance to Catholicism may grow out of one's ethnic background. Very often these folks will fight you tooth and nail if you suggest that their Catholicism is somehow deficient; meanwhile, they seldom read the Bible, go to Mass, share their faith, or ever visit a priest. Once again, we need to point out that Protestants are just as guilty of this. "I'm Baptist." Why? "I'm from Kentucky, what do you think I'd be?" (With all due respect to my friends from Kentucky.) In both cases, it's necessary to help our loved ones to see that following Christ is much more than being part of a certain ethnicity or demographic. The way to do this is not to jump down their throats. Rather, demonstrate how Jesus meaningfully defines every facet of your life and pray that your example will lead your friend to honest self-evaluation. In time, God may provide opportunity for you to explain the reason for your hope in Christ.
- People may state that truth is socially constructed and relative, but no one lives that way consistently. The saying that there are no atheists in foxholes is true. Inevitably life presents us with circumstances that exceed our resources and cause us to look honestly toward God. It may be years before your friends reach this place, but the day will come, you can be sure. Pray that as you continue to exemplify the life of Christ,

they will see you as a reliable friend in whom they can confide when the day of trial comes.

While visiting Italy, I taught in an Evangelical church. After presenting a particular lesson, a nun with a bright smile named Idana approached me to express her gratitude. I later learned from my host that Idana had undergone a conversion of sorts and is now an excellent student of the Bible. In her lifetime as a Catholic nun, she has identified with each of the categories we have discussed. She served in ministry before Vatican II and is still going strong forty years later. Most recently she has been influenced by an Evangelical missionary. The following excerpt is taken from her testimony, which she graciously wrote down for us. As you read it, take note of how her convictions center on the Evangelical priorities of Scripture and personal relationship with God:

> March 2008
>
> Here is a brief reflection on my encounter with the Word of God. I am a nun in northern Italy. As a result of precious friendship with an Evangelical church in our city, I am now different. I carry in my heart attention to God's Word and an increasing longing to know it. I find religious rituals such as the homilies of our priests to be insufficient. They do not possess the personal exchange of truth which is both simpler and more conducive to loving God.
>
> Today I count myself blessed. A few hours a week I have opportunity to interact with my Evangelical friend. God has used her to show me that his written Word is the authority that brings joy. It is necessary to give priority to the Bible and study it every day so as to become familiar with it, ready to handle it in the various problems that are posed in daily life. It must come forth spontaneously, flowing from our heart and intellect, the right citation at just the right time. This is my great desire. I wait for God to speak through his Word.

I believe that the Bible interprets itself with the Bible: this is the key, the central way in which God's truth should be applied. At this point our faith becomes both objective and subjective: objective because it is based on the Rock, which is Christ Jesus; subjective because it is appropriated in our personal experience. It is precisely living in this tension of interaction between the Creator and the creature that we realize greater intimacy with Jesus, the God-man.

I am interested in theology, and particularly the theme of eternal life. "He who has the Son, has life" (1 John 5:12); "For God so loved the word that he gave his only Son, that whoever believes in him will not die but have eternal life" (John 3:16). "Truly, truly I tell you: whoever hears my words and believes in him who sent me, has eternal life. He does not come into judgment, but has passed from death to life" (John 5:24).

Thank you for the friendship which has offered me this opportunity for exchange, so as to penetrate God's Word, which is our gift and joy.

In fede,
Sr. Idana

Some will find our three profiles of Catholics overly narrow. They might like to point out additional forms of Catholicism, such as Latino spirituality, mystic devotion, or proponents of social justice. This is a valid observation. However, even in these instances, the three profiles apply. For instance, there are Latino Catholics for whom the traditional emphasis on Our Lady of Guadalupe is everything. Other Latinos are more Bible oriented. And there are still others whose Catholicism doesn't reach farther than the gold cross around their necks, as in the cultural Catholic. While the particular details and beliefs of Catholics within each of the profiles will vary, the basic authority to which they subscribe generally boils down to one of the big three: traditional, Evangelical, or cultural.

I think that Catholic journalist Peter Feuerherd has said it well: "Religious reality is complicated, and why people do what they do with their spiritual lives comes from a complex meshing of tradition, culture, and personal choice."[8] On account of this reality, we must have a missionary mindset toward our Catholic friends and family members. This missional perspective will prepare us to relate to them with a proper balance of grace and truth. In the next chapter we will consider how we can realize this elusive balance.

8. Feuerherd, *Holyland USA*, 83.

Chapter 11

HOW TO RELATE TO CATHOLICS WITH GRACE AND TRUTH

Walking across a bridge, I saw a man on the edge preparing to jump. I ran over and said, "Stop. Don't do it."

"Why not?" he asked.

"Well, there's so much to live for!"

"Like what?"

"Are you religious?"

He said, "Yes."

I said, "Me too. Are you a Christian or Buddhist?"

"Christian."

"Me too. Are you Catholic or Protestant?"

"Protestant."

"Me too. Are you Episcopalian or Baptist?"

"Baptist."

"Me too. Are you Baptist Church of God or Church of the Lord?"

"Baptist Church of God."

> "Me too! Are you Reformed Baptist Church of God, Reformation of 1879, or Reformed Baptist Church of God, Reformation of 1915?"
>
> He said, "Reformed of 1915."
>
> I said, "Die, heretic scum," and pushed him off.[1]

This joke has circulated for many years as an example of Protestant dogmatism at its worst. It is still around because, sadly, it contains a bit of truth. Sometimes one will defend this behavior by quoting a biblical text like Jude 3, "Contend for the faith that was once for all entrusted to the saints." As urgent as it is for us to maintain right doctrine, Evangelical polemics too infrequently balance love for people (1 Tim. 1:5) and commitment to preserving unity (Eph. 4:3).[2]

Please don't get me wrong; I'm not suggesting that we should be so open-minded that our brains fall out of our heads. We must also be discerning, as Paul says in Philippians, "And this is my prayer: that your love may abound more and more in knowledge and depth of insight, so that you may be able to discern what is best" (Phil. 1:9–10). And if we're going to be critical about anything, may it be the message of Jesus' death and resurrection (Gal. 1:1–9). What I want to critique is the combative posture that goes directly for the jugular of any poor soul who may disagree with our particular view. To my embarrassment, I have been guilty of this more than once.

FAMILY FEUD

Returning home to New York after my first year at Moody Bible Institute, I managed to alienate myself from more than a few Catholic friends and family members. My intention was genuine, but in retro-

1. James B. Twitchell, *Shopping for God: How Christianity Went from in Your Heart to in Your Face* (New York: Simon and Schuster, 2007), 113–14.
2. You might also consider Matt. 13:30: "Let both [wheat and tares] grow together until the harvest. At that time I will tell the harvesters: First collect the weeds and tie them in bundles to be burned; then gather the wheat and bring it into my barn," or the words of Jesus when he said, "Whoever is not against us is for us" (Mark 9:40).

spect I realize that I behaved like a doctrinal pit bull. The reason for my stupidity is captured by the word *sophomore*. This word, which describes the second year of university study, comes from two Greek words: *sophos*, meaning "wise," and *moros*, meaning "fool" (or more literally, "moron"). It is a time period that the German theologian Helmut Thielicke called "theological puberty," a typical phase in the development of every student in which one's knowledge exceeds his spiritual maturity.

While attending Moody, I accompanied a professor and some classmates to a three-day conference in Dallas titled "Ex-Catholics for Christ." It was held at a large suburban Bible church and attracted former Catholics from around the country. The daily lineup of lessons was predictable: Bible teachers explained a biblical text (mostly from Galatians) or lectured about an event from the Protestant Reformation. In more than one session the pope was described negatively using the book of Revelation.

At the end of the second day, something caught my attention. I overheard a couple of guest speakers discussing what they called the "apostasy" of certain Christian leaders for having signed the ecumenical document "Evangelicals and Catholics Together." Perhaps the most disturbing part was the condescending tone with which they spoke. I soon heard the same invective aspersions cast by others. It then dawned on me that, with a few exceptions, this chorus of dissent had been expressed throughout much of the conference. While I agreed with many of their theological concerns, I was appalled by their condemning spirit. It became disturbing to the point that I considered going out to find a Catholic clerical collar to wear in the plenary session just to see how individuals would respond in the face of a living and breathing person. Self-control prevailed.

After completing my studies at Moody, my new bride and I moved to New England so I could begin a master's of divinity at Gordon-Conwell Theological Seminary. One of the extraordinary features of Gordon-Conwell is the so-called Boston Theological Institute (BTI).

BTI is a consortium of nine divinity schools in the Boston area in which enrollment is open to students who choose to participate. The most memorable class I took through BTI was at Harvard Divinity School with visiting professor N. T. Wright (a British New Testament scholar). In addition to taking in Wright's lectures, students met in hour-long breakout sessions following each class.

If I were to describe the profile of our breakout meetings with one word, it would be *eclectic*. This variety was partially a function of Harvard; the other reason was probably the popularity of Professor Wright. Whatever the cause, students came from a wide range of religious backgrounds.

In one session, our student leader started with a fascinating statement. She said, "All religions of the world seek to answer the question, 'How can I be saved?' We may define 'saved' differently; nonetheless, we all share a desire to be delivered from one state of affairs unto a greater level of existence." She then pointed to various students around the table and asked them to provide an answer to her question from the vantage point of their religious tradition. What came next I shall never forget.

"Enkyo, how would you answer the question?"

Enkyo closed his eyes and spoke in his typical soft voice. "Buddhism says that we suffer because our base desires crave that which is temporary. The solution to this is to cease all desire in order to realize the nonexistence of the self, otherwise known as nirvana."

"Gloria, how would you answer?"

Gloria was a young woman who was less than fond of the male gender. She thought for a moment and responded, "God, the divine Mother nourishes her creation with the milk of her cosmic spirit. We will observe salvation when humanity stops discriminating on the basis of biologically determined qualities like sex."

"Vishnu, how would you answer the question?"

Vishnu was evidently preparing his answer while the others spoke, because he quickly retorted without a pause, "As Hindus, we believe that, by nature, man is good and made of the same essence of the divine. Man's problem is that he is ignorant of his divine nature. We must realize our divinity and must then strive to detach ourselves from selfish desires in order to attain enlightenment."

"Peter, how would you answer the question?"

Peter, a Catholic student, thought for a moment, then simply recited the Apostles' Creed, "I believe in God, the Father Almighty, the Creator of heaven and earth, and in Jesus Christ, His only Son, our Lord: Who was conceived of the Holy Spirit, born of the Virgin Mary, suffered under Pontius Pilate, was crucified, died, and was buried. He descended into hell. The third day He arose again from the dead. He ascended into heaven and sits at the right hand of God the Father Almighty, whence he shall come to judge the living and the dead. I believe in the Holy Spirit, the holy catholic church, the communion of saints, the forgiveness of sins, the resurrection of the body, and life everlasting. Amen."

His answer grabbed me, for it was the one that I would have given.

From Peter's answer, I learned a profound lesson. While there are many important doctrines that divide Catholics and Evangelicals, there is also much on which we agree (for example, the Apostles' Creed and the Nicene Creed). This little incident helped me see our similarities in ways I hadn't previously. This same insight would surface several more times before the end of the semester. For instance, as our class debated the veracity of Jesus' resurrection, Peter and his fellow PhD students from Boston College offered crushing arguments against our liberal Protestant classmates. Not only did Peter provide compelling refutations to those who denied the empty tomb, he also explained the resurrection in ways that stirred the soul. Despite significant doctrinal differences, these Catholic scholars were our allies in theological debate and, equally important, our brothers and sisters in Christ.

HOW WE VIEW CATHOLICS

Some readers have just thrown their copy of this book against the wall and yelled something containing the words *ecumenical* and *lunatic.*

This is good. You need to get it out of your system. But before you consign me to the heretical society of Judas, Arius, and Pelagius, let me explain further.

Among Evangelicals there are a variety of ways to view Catholics. Our particular view naturally informs how we consider and relate to them. Some feel called to shove Catholics off the proverbial bridge. Others swim down the river clinching a life preserver with their teeth. Whichever position you might hold, it's important to be conscious of it; otherwise you'll be throwing books across the room without knowing why.

A friend of mine named Jim Hatcher has created a most helpful tool for evaluating the different ways that Evangelicals view Catholics. Having served in Austria for many years, he is well acquainted with the nuances of these positions. As you read through his outline, consider which category best describes you.

EVANGELICALS AND ROMAN CATHOLICS
A TAXONOMY OF EVANGELICAL APPROACHES

Actively anti–Roman Catholic	Evangelicals with an actively anti–Roman Catholic approach have a strong focus on the teaching and practices of the Roman Catholic Church which they feel are contrary to biblical teaching. The errors of these teachings and practices are felt to be so substantial and fundamental that most Evangelicals with this approach feel it is virtually impossible to be both a born-again Christian and a practicing member of the Roman Catholic Church. Churches and individuals with this approach feel that it is important to regularly and decisively explain these differences. Contact with Roman Catholics is generally limited to evangelizing them and public polemic, in which the perceived errors of Roman Catholic teaching and practice are exposed.

Passively anti–Roman Catholic	Evangelicals with a passively anti–Roman Catholic approach share the convictions of those who are actively anti–Roman Catholic concerning the teachings and practices of the Roman Catholic Church. They generally do not, however, use the public square to critique those teachings and practices. While there tends to be a strong desire to clarify distinctives among themselves, contact with Roman Catholic institutions is avoided and contact with Roman Catholic members is generally limited to evangelism.
Coexistent	Those Evangelicals with a coexistent approach are concerned not to antagonize Roman Catholics by openly criticizing the Roman Catholic Church, its teachings, or its practices. Many Evangelicals with this approach rarely concern themselves with doctrinal issues of any sort, including those that relate to Catholics. When differences are evident, they are seldom addressed. Their posture is best described as ambivalent.
Positive identity	Evangelicals with a positive-identity approach to Roman Catholics are relatively open about their distinctives, while avoiding criticism of the Roman Catholic Church. They seek common ground as well as positive contact with Roman Catholics and Roman Catholic institutions. While cautious, they are open to cooperating with Roman Catholics in isolated social projects such as pro-life efforts and disaster relief. They hesitate, however, to cooperate evangelistically, since they reject both the institution and authority of the Roman Catholic Church as well as certain central doctrines. Less central differences, as perceived by these Evangelicals, tend to be minimized.
Symbiotic	Evangelicals with a symbiotic approach, while maintaining core distinctives, welcome and may even seek cooperation with Roman Catholics on multiple fronts. As with the

	coexistent approach, differences are seldom the subject of internal teaching or public debate. By contrast, however, resources and energy are expended to actively pursue positive points of contact, publicly underscoring common beliefs and practices and supporting common causes. This would include cooperation with "believing" Catholics in evangelistic efforts. Evangelicals with this approach do not want to be perceived as competing with Roman Catholic institutions.
Ecumenical	Evangelicals with an ecumenical approach seek to build bridges with Roman Catholics in pursuit of unity. Evangelism among active Roman Catholics is discouraged and common ground is the subject of both public proclamation and in-house teaching. Differences are generally perceived to be a matter of preference, historical and cultural, rather than as theological and fundamental matters. Evangelicals with this approach make full use of Roman Catholic institutions and other interconfessional structures.
Internal renewal	Evangelicals with an internal-renewal approach toward Roman Catholics seek to work within the Roman Catholic Church and its institutions. Their desire is to encourage renewal with the goal of restoring "prodigal" Roman Catholics both to personal faith and to the Roman Catholic Church. Their focus is often evangelism and personal discipleship through Bible study under the authority of, or at least in cooperation with, the local Roman Catholic priest and parish. Divisive distinctions in teaching or practice are avoided or minimized.

"Evangelicals" are here defined as Protestant Christians who agree with the "Basis of Faith" of the European Evangelical Alliance. Used with permission from James Hatcher.

Maybe you're wondering which category I fit into. Overall, I resonate most with the positive identity position. Readers who also identify with this category (along with the symbiotic position) are enjoying this book and will recommend it to their friends. The actively anti-Catholic readers are probably frustrated. Some of them are looking for an email address or a website in order to write me a scathing message complete with references to the bowl judgments of Revelation and the lake of fire. The ecumenical or internal renewal reader thinks that I wear my theological underwear a little too tight. "Relax," they say. "We're in the twenty-first century. It's no longer about doctrine; it's about love, baby. Get rid of your modernist habit of trying to define truth, and you'll realize that the Reformation is over."

I'm not hung up on the terminology, but I believe that the position Hatcher calls positive identity is preferable because it seeks to uphold a distinctively Evangelical understanding of redemption[3] (hence limited cooperation in evangelism) while simultaneously acknowledging the meaningful agreement between Catholics and Evangelicals (particularly in the realm of social outreach).[4] A balance of this sort is necessary. As mentioned earlier, Jesus embodied and expressed a balance of "grace *and* truth" (John 1:14, emphasis added). As Christ's followers, we the church are called to do the same. Not everyone will slice the onion exactly the same way, but slice it we must. If we toss out the entire onion or consume it whole, we've failed to do the hard work of upholding both virtues.

In my role as a pastor, I often observe how personalities lean toward one or the other poles, grace *or* truth. Some of us naturally resemble lambs; others are more like pit bulls. That's life in a world full of uniquely created people. Consequently, we shouldn't be surprised when we disagree on how to handle specific issues, but such disagreement

---

3. See chapter 8 for an explanation of where the Catholic and Evangelical views of salvation differ.
4. I have in mind the context of the United States. Other parts of the world, like Italy or Latin America, for instance, may function much differently in this regard and thus preclude the sort of partnership that is possible in North America.

shouldn't undermine the enterprise of trying to thoughtfully navigate through our differences. Although we must agree to disagree in some places, courteous dialog is a much more Christian approach than throwing polemical hand grenades over the ecclesial fence.

One of the reasons why Evangelical Christians fail to engage the process of balancing grace and truth among Catholics is overconfidence coupled with a lack of respect for the other person. In his book *Humble Apologetics*, author John Stackhouse elucidates this idea:

> To put it more sharply, we should sound like we really do respect the intelligence and spiritual interest and moral integrity of our neighbors. We should act as if we do see the very image of God in them.... It is a voice that speaks authentically out of Christian convictions about our own very real limitations and our neighbor's very real dignity, not cynical expediency. We are rhetorically humble because we are *not* prophets infallibly inspired by God, let alone the One who could speak "with authority" in a way no one else can speak. We are mere messengers of that One: messengers who earnestly mean well, but who forget this bit of the message or never really understood that bit; messengers who never entirely live up to their own good news; messengers who recognize the ambiguities in the world that make the message harder to believe; and therefore messengers who can sympathize with neighbors who aren't ready just yet to believe everything we're telling them.[5]

Being humble doesn't mean that we have compromised our conviction of what constitutes truth any more than being meek suggests that one is devoid of strength. Jesus was all powerful, and yet he humbled himself to the point of death, even death on a cross (Phil. 2:1–11). It's only when we have an informed conviction, having taken

5. John G. Stackhouse Jr., *Humble Apologetics: Defending the Faith Today* (Oxford: Oxford Univ. Press, 2002), 229.

time to listen, learn, and think, that we possess the requisite courage to relate to others in a vulnerable, humble way. Conversely, when we attack the one who disagrees with us, we demonstrate our insecurity. Once again, Jesus is our example. Although God, Jesus did not exploit his deity but made himself nothing, taking the form of a servant (Phil. 2:6–7). This is indeed the Christian way.

So far this chapter has been concerned with acquiring a biblical, Jesus-centered perspective on Catholicism. In a sense that's half the equation. Once we learn to look at Catholics through the eyes of Jesus, we effectively communicate with them in light of their particular values and priorities.

COMMUNICATING WITH CATHOLICS ABOUT THE GOSPEL

Talking to someone about the gospel is evangelism. In my role as pastor of outreach, I often hear people describe evangelism differently. To clarify its meaning, the following definition and subsequent unpacking of it will get us started:

> Evangelism is the activity in which the entire church prayerfully and intentionally relies on God in sharing gospel love and truth, in order to bring people one step closer to Jesus Christ.

The entire church. The church is the body of Christ. As such, we extend hope to the world by communicating the message of Jesus' death and resurrection. Gospel outreach is not simply one ministry option among many, something that only a gifted evangelist does. Rather, sharing Christ strikes at the heart of who we are. Just as Jesus is the light of the world, who in his very being shines the hope of salvation, so we, in Christ, are the same. In this way, gospel activity is central to our identity, much as heat is a natural extension of the sun's rays. This evangelistic call applies to every Christian, from the youngest to the oldest.

Prayerfully. Talking to God in prayer relates to every facet of the evangelistic enterprise. Prayer provides wisdom to the evangelist; it appropriates power for its proclamation; and, in some mysterious way, God uses it to accomplish his redemptive purposes. Prayer is also the common denominator of every renewal movement in the history of Christ's church.

Intentionally. Evangelism happens with intentionality. Having been inspired, equipped, and mobilized by church leaders, the congregation is positioned to seize gospel opportunities. For example, at a nearby mall, I recently observed a young girl walking up a downward-moving escalator. As soon as the child stopped walking, she immediately began heading downward. With additional steps, however, she continued moving up. This illustration helps me think about the challenge to maintain gospel outreach. The busyness of life and the gravity of selfishness draw us downward. To the extent that we are intentional, evangelism has potential to make progress.

Relying on God. Psalm 18:2 says, "The Lord is my rock, my fortress and my deliverer; my God is my rock, in whom I take refuge. He is my shield, and the horn of my salvation, my stronghold" (ESV). The psalmist is intent on exalting God as the foundation of his salvation and does so by choosing eight different ways to say it. In the Hebrew language, indeed in any language, this manner of repetition emphatically underscores the point: salvation is of God! Because of this great truth, we can joyfully and confidently rely on him.

In revealing gospel love and truth. Being a Christian is more than being a friendly person. I have the privilege of knowing some nice people. My colleague Jay Thomas, for instance, always appears to be happy. What's more, his joy is contagious. If you asked him, he would tell you that his positive attitude is an outgrowth of his faith. However, I suspect that no one has ever looked at Jay and concluded, "Wow, he is a nice guy! I'll bet Jesus died for my sins and rose from the dead to provide me with forgiveness and eternal life." This kind of inference doesn't come from abstract deduction; it requires explanation. For outreach to be more than friendly service, we must communicate gospel content.

To bring people. Notice, it doesn't say "to bring unbelievers"; it says to bring "people." As I explained earlier, evangelism — the activity of sharing the gospel — is bigger than just conversion. After initially coming to Christ, we still need the gospel to liberate us from sin and establish us in righteousness. Thus, to say that we evangelize someone doesn't mean that the recipient is necessarily without faith.

At the same time, those outside of Christ are in dire need of the gospel. This need provides much of the motivation for evangelistic outreach. Consequently, we who have been in the church for a while must break out from our holy huddles. Like Jesus — the friend of tax collectors and sinners — we must forge meaningful relationships with nonbelievers. In Jesus' words, "You are the light of the world. A city set on a hill cannot be hidden" (Matt. 5:14).

One step closer to Christ. Of all the points I've made so far, this is the one I am most passionate about. Sometimes we define evangelism by a particular method. For many of us, it's the crusade approach made popular by D. L. Moody or, more recently, Billy Graham. Accordingly, we think of evangelism as a full-blown gospel presentation that begins by explaining the human problem of sin and culminates in an invitation for one to receive Christ.

I don't know about you, but most of my gospel encounters don't allow for a full-orbed sermon. In a crusade, the goal of the evangelist is to clearly present the entire message and urge someone to make a decision. (It's probably not an accident that the Billy Graham Evangelistic Association's magazine is named *Decision*.) However, if you define all evangelism that way, what happens when you have only two minutes to talk to a colleague beside the water cooler during break? How do you witness to the checkout person in the supermarket, or to a family member who knows what you believe and is utterly disinterested in hearing any more sermons? The answer is — you don't. You don't say a thing. We can't share in that kind of way without alienating people; therefore, we don't share at all. The outcome is the same as hiding our lamps beneath the proverbial table. What we need to learn is how to gradually plant seeds of gospel truth that help people incrementally move one step closer to Christ. Therefore, instead of defining evangelism strictly as a comprehensive presentation of the "full delmonte" (everything there is to say about salvation) culminating in a Billy Graham–like invitation, we need to view the incremental efforts of seed planting, which we perform in the course of natural relationships, as not only a legitimate form of evangelism but also a critical method among our Catholic loved ones.

■■■

Once we understand the meaning of the word *evangelism*, we can start to reflect on how to actually do it. The how-to question must be informed by the particular context in which one is operating. Therefore, we will conclude this chapter by considering how we can minister the gospel in the context of our Catholic friends and family.

In the interest of bringing some organization to the following principles, I've put them into a simple framework. Using the metaphor of a traffic light, we will look at the red-light (habits that must stop), yellow-light (areas of caution), and green-light (good regular practices) approaches to evangelism. Assuming that Evangelicals eat their vitamins and get regular eye exams, these colors will help us to steer through relational intersections with more effectiveness.

RED LIGHT

Don't Be a Pit Bull

In our zeal to defend biblical teaching, we sometimes approach Catholics with an adversarial posture. Instead of manifesting the love of Jesus, we are like foaming-at-the-mouth pit bulls. It's critical that we remember Jesus' words from Matthew 22:37–39: " 'Love the Lord your God with all your heart and with all your soul and with all your mind.' This is the first and greatest commandment. And the second is like it: 'Love your neighbor as yourself.'" Have you ever wondered why the second commandment is like the first? It's because people are made in God's image and therefore deserve the utmost respect.[6] Instead of listening only so far as it helps us plot our next incendiary retort, biblical love is committed to listening with a humble posture, to understand and to bless the other.

Don't Attempt to Debate People into the Kingdom

When we communicate the gospel to Catholics, we often make the mistake of thinking that our conversations should directly address doctrinal issues. This is not only incorrect, it is impossible. When speaking to a friend about faith, we don't speak directly to his religious beliefs; we speak to a *person* who holds religious beliefs. This is a crucial distinction which we often overlook. Stackhouse puts his finger on it: "To put it starkly, if 'message without life' was sufficient, Christ didn't need to perform signs, nor did he need to form personal relationships in which to teach the gospel to those who would believe him and spread the word. He could simply have hired scribes to write down his message and distribute it."[7]

Frankly, this is what frustrates me about most books written to equip Evangelicals on how to discuss faith with Catholics. They seem to assume that if you can simply pile up enough proofs, Catholics will have no choice but to surrender under the weight of your argument. Sure, we must have reliable evidence and must know how to marshal it effectively, but we can't ignore the personal dynamics which make up our communication (things like credibility, personal integrity, and the amalgamation of Catholic religion with one's cultural or ethnic identity). For more on these dynamics and how to navigate through them, review the profiles in chapter 10.

6. Similarly, the apostle Paul describes the nature of true love in 1 Corinthians 13 when he says that it "bears all things, believes all things, hopes all things, endures all things" (NASB).

7. Stackhouse, *Humble Apologetics*, 134.

Don't Partake of the Mass

If you are attending a Mass for some reason, we who were once Catholic are sometimes tempted to receive Communion. You may have spent much of your life receiving it, and in many circumstances getting in the Eucharist line may avoid awkwardness with Catholic family or friends. What we must realize, however, is that from the Catholic Church's point of view, we are not in communion with her and therefore it is inappropriate to partake. Furthermore, receiving the host sends a mixed message to our Catholic friends, because in their eyes partaking is tantamount to affirming that the wafer is indeed the body of Christ. (This is precisely what you say before the priest puts it on your tongue or in your hand.) For these reasons it is appropriate to abstain.

YELLOW LIGHT

Be Cautious of How You Use Language

Sometimes we make the mistake of thinking that because we employ the same terminology, we share a common understanding of what such words mean. The following is a list of the slippery terms that regularly undermine our communication with Catholic friends and family.

Anointing: Catholics often associate *anointing* with the sacrament of confirmation. It is also a liturgical element of baptism and holy orders (ordination). Many Evangelicals, particularly from the charismatic tradition, use the term *anointing* to describe spiritual empowerment that is possessed and expressed by one who serves the gospel.

Baptism: For Catholics this is the first of the seven sacraments. It is believed to remove guilt and impart spiritual life. Water is poured on the head while a minister pronounces the Trinitarian invocation: "the Father, the Son, and the Holy Spirit." Most Evangelicals regard baptism to be a sacrament (or ordinance) which signifies identification with Christ without actually causing spiritual transformation.

Body of Christ: When Catholics speak of "Christ's body," they likely refer to the sacramental presence of Jesus Christ in the Eucharist under the appearances of bread and wine. Evangelicals, on the other hand, typically think of God's people, the church.

Church: Catholics recognize three inseparable uses of the word *church*: the worldwide union of God's people, a regional assembly (diocese), and a local parish (which gathers to celebrate the Eucharist). Very often Catholics will use the word *church* to describe the building or facility in which God's people meet for worship. While agreeing with the three designations for God's people (universal, regional, and local), Evangelicals are in principle reticent to use the word *church* in relation to the building.

Communion: Among Catholics, communion is the union of God's people to Christ and to one another with its "source and summit in the celebration of the Eucharist."[8] The Evangelical view of Eucharist is different in that we don't assign to it the same sacramental function vis-a-vis transubstantiation.

Confession: Catholics see confession as a critical element of the sacrament of penance and reconciliation. It is associated with telling one's sins to a priest, although it seems that few Catholics today maintain this routine. Evangelicals will tell their sins directly to God in prayer, or perhaps with a fellow believer in the context of an accountability relationship.

Word of God: Catholics understand God's Word to be the revelation of Jesus Christ contained in Scripture *and* Sacred Tradition. Evangelicals tend to think of the Bible when talking about the Word of God.

Gospel: The gospel is the good news of salvation in Jesus Christ. Often Catholics will think of the apostolic deposit of faith or the four books of the New Testament called the Gospels. Evangelicals are more likely to use the word to describe the message that is preached or shared in the context of personal evangelism.

Prayer: Notwithstanding Evangelical Catholics, most Catholic prayers are usually written down in advance or read from a card or

8. *Catechism of the Catholic Church*, 871.

book. Furthermore, Catholic prayers could be directed to any number of saints. Evangelicals usually don't read prayers. They tend to be spontaneous and directed to God alone in Jesus' name.

Religion: For Catholics this is a positive word. It describes the tangible forms of faith in which God and humanity relate. Among Evangelicals it has the connotation of mechanical rituals by which one attempts to merit salvation. In fact, it's common to hear Evangelicals promote relationship with God rather than religion.[9]

Repentance: Catholics use this word as they do *contrition* and *reconciliation*, as a necessary ingredient for the reception of the sacrament of penance. Instead of associating it with a sacrament, Evangelicals often see repentance as a component of conversion (as in "repentance and faith").

Salvation: The Catholic Church defines salvation as "the forgiveness of sins and restoration of friendship with God, which can be done by God alone."[10] The particular way God does this is through the sacramental system, which is what most Catholics think of when they hear the word *salvation*. (The Evangelical Catholic will differ here.) Thus, salvation is understood to span the entirety of life, from the infant's baptismal font to the grave. Evangelicals, on the other hand, commonly use *salvation* as a synonym for *justification*—the moment when one enters into favor with God. This difference is partly why Catholics are incredulous when we talk about "being saved." Since they regard salvation to happen over a lifetime, they wonder, "How can anyone possibly know the answer before they die and undergo judgment?"

Sin: The Catholic Church teaches that sin is "an offense against God as well as a fault against reason, truth, and right conscience. Sin is a deliberate thought, word, deed, or omission contrary to the eternal law of God. In judging the gravity of sin, it is customary to distinguish

9. Evangelicals would do well to remember, however, that Scripture uses the term *religion*. As it says in James 1:27, "Religion that God our Father accepts as pure and faultless is this: to look after orphans and widows in their distress and to keep oneself from being polluted by the world."

10. *Catechism of the Catholic Church*, 898.

between mortal and venial sins."[11] As this definition emphasizes, when Catholics speak of sin, they have in mind the wrong actions that one commits. Evangelicals tend to stress the fallen nature which gives rise to these moral failures (to "fall short of the glory of God" [Rom. 3:23]).

Sunday school: When Catholics hear this term, they usually think of a class for children, not for adults. If you tell them about your experience in Sunday school (as an adult), don't be surprised if you see puzzled expressions.

■■■

Some Evangelical words are foreign to Catholic ears. Usually, Catholics don't talk about being "saved" or "born again" (notwithstanding the Evangelical Catholic). If a traditional or cultural Catholic speaks this way, he will likely have infant baptism in mind. Likewise, it's unlikely you'll hear the words witness, devotions (or devotionals), fellowship, believer, small group, evangelism, or quiet time. In short, it's wise to avoid tribal language that's unique to one's Evangelical circle but incomprehensible to outsiders.

Other things we say can be unintentionally offensive. For example, it is axiomatic for Evangelicals to describe themselves as Christian as opposed to those who are Catholic. We don't realize that to many, this dichotomy sounds like we're putting Catholics into a non-Christian category. I once heard a student of Wheaton College talk this way to Archbishop Cardinal Francis George. The cardinal was less than impressed. What makes this situation tricky is that some Catholics also use this distinction. My suggestion is to err on the side of caution by not juxtaposing Christian and Catholic.

Recognize Your Familial Position

Communication with family is especially difficult. It was a challenge for Jesus. The Lord says in Matthew 13:57, "Only in his hometown

11. Ibid., 899.

and in his own house is a prophet without honor." In context, Jesus is referring to the people among whom he grew up, including family, who had difficulty receiving his message. This isn't surprising; familiarity breeds contempt.

It helps to understand the position you hold in your family. Your aunt Louise who used to change your diaper when you were an infant is probably not immediately disposed to learning from you about God. Even though you've earned your MDiv and PhD in theology and have been a pastor for over twenty years, at one level she still sees you as the little kid who used to drool on himself. We must identify these relational obstacles and pray for God's wisdom to handle them properly.

Be Cautious of Emotional Intensity

When we discuss faith with Catholics, our conversation tends to be so freighted with emotion that it is practically doomed from the start, especially in families where there has been a history of disagreement on such issues. This is so largely because unlike Evangelical belief, which often centers on doctrinal propositions, Catholic commitment includes a full-orbed culture, including one's personal, familial, and ethnic histories. Because these commitments run deep into one's identity, questions about the veracity of Catholic claims simultaneously address the larger culture into which those views are woven. The potential for emotional combustion in this scenario can't be overestimated.

GREEN LIGHT

Engage in Gospel Dialog

In some circles *dialog* is a dirty word. It's considered to be the second cousin of the term *ecumenism*, which Evangelicals sometimes use synonymously for religious compromise. There are reasons why these connections are made. (Ecumenism in the liberal world gave up on a supernatural gospel a long time ago.) Nevertheless, to regard these terms as synonyms is unwarranted. A humble exchange of ideas need not be antithetical to gospel conviction.

Several months ago I attended the funeral of a priest. A good friend of mine is a Jewish woman who had earned her PhD under this Catholic scholar. Because the priest had a small family, there were only five of the six men needed to carry the casket. They asked me to be the final pall bearer (probably because I was wearing a black suit); I gladly obliged.

The event was an example of ecumenism—a Jewish woman giving the homily and a Protestant pastor carrying the body of a Catholic priest. The dialog happened afterward at an upscale Irish pub. The fellow seated beside me was seriously Catholic. I know this because he said so. In the same breath he also tried to recruit me to join the Knights of Columbus. During the hour of our conversation, we covered most of the issues in this book. (It's hard to turn research mode off.) By the time this gentleman started to drink his fourth glass of Guinness, the value of his input had waned. Nevertheless, the interchange was insightful.

When I talk about conducting dialog, I'm not promoting conversation for its own sake. We do it as evangelism; we seek to convey the gospel message in the hope of seeing the person with whom we're speaking (and ourselves) drawn closer to Jesus. Since evangelism is based upon objective truth claims, dialog ought to involve a real interchange of beliefs and not a superficial, you're-okay-I'm-okay session. I like how the late Richard John Neuhaus has put it: "Our unity in the truth is more evident in our quarreling about the truth than in our settling for something less than the truth. At the same time we recognize that, short of the end time, none of us possesses the truth entirely, exhaustively and without remainder. Such possession awaits the consummation when, as Paul says in 1 Corinthians 13, we know even as we are known."[12]

12. Richard John Neuhaus, "A New Thing: Ecumenism at the Threshold of the Third Millennium," in *Reclaiming the Great Tradition*, ed. James S. Cutsinger (Downers Grove, IL: InterVarsity, 1997), 58. See also Pope Benedict XVI's comments in Joseph Cardinal Ratzinger, *Principles of Catholic Theology: Building Stones for Fundamental Theology*, trans. Sr. Mary Frances McCarthy, S.N.D. (San Francisco: Ignatius, 1987), 236.

Ecumenical dialog that is principled with a clear gospel objective presents the opportunity to advance Christ's kingdom.

Keep the Main Thing the Main Thing

When talking with Catholics, there are myriad potential rabbit trails. We may enter into a conversation to talk about how Jesus provides life with meaning and suddenly find ourselves enmeshed in a debate about the Apocrypha or *Humanae vitae.* Sometimes it's right to broach these subjects, but too often we do so at the expense of the gospel. This is a travesty! What does it profit a person if he explicates a host of theological conundrums without focusing attention upon the death and resurrection of Jesus? This, I would contend, is the main thing—bearing witness to the splendor and majesty of our Savior, the one who died, rose, and now lives.

The implications of understanding the main thing are significant. For starters, it means that I'm more concerned with friends and relatives trusting fully in Jesus than in their leaving their Catholic parish. As mentioned earlier, because Catholicism represents a deep and complex culture including familial and ethnic allegiances, it's sometimes unrealistic to think that older relatives will immediately say goodbye to their church for an Evangelical congregation. Personally, I'm not going to insist that such people demonstrate their commitment to Christ by exiting the Catholic community. I'd much rather provide biblical resources and encouragement to help them grow in their faith, trusting that in God's timing they will look to the Bible to sort out questions of church membership and participation.

The sort of attitude that I'm promoting in relation to Catholic family and friends was appropriately expressed by C. S. Lewis. On one occasion he wrote a letter to a female friend who had converted to Catholicism. His words provide an example of how to extend love in the face of disagreement. "It is a little difficult to explain how I feel that though you have taken a way which is not for me, I nevertheless can congratulate you—I suppose because of your faith and joy which are so obviously increased. Naturally, I do not draw from that the same conclusions as you—but there is no need for us to start a controversial correspondence! I believe that we are very dear to one another but not because I am at all on the Rome-ward frontier of my own communion. I believe that in the present divided state of Christendom, those who are at the heart of each division are closer to one another than those who are at the fringes."[13]

To some, the words of Lewis are a scandalous compromise, a bold denial of truth. It seems to me, however, that they express genuine respect and affection for his friend. If we trust in God's sovereignty and believe in the power of prayer, we can look forward to a day when we engage in doctrinal discussion and debate, but hopefully not in the absence of authentic relationship.

If we are to have a reasonable chance at realizing authentic relationship with our Catholic family and friends, we must capture a biblical vision of Jesus Christ. This is what we'll look at in the next chapter.

---

13. Quoted by Timothy George, "Evangelicals and the Great Tradition," *First Things*, no. 175 (August/September 2007), 21.

Chapter 12

GLORIFY GOD AND ENJOY HIM FOREVER

"Hail to Dorothy, the Wicked Witch is dead!" With a simple bucket of water, Dorothy slew the dreaded witch, and it didn't come a moment too soon. My six-year-old heart was about to beat out of my chest. But thanks to the strategically located bucket, disaster was evaded — until the next scene. After obtaining the witch's broomstick, Dorothy strolled into the wizard's throne room hoping to find a way home. The gigantic head of the wizard responded by hollering orders amid flames, smoke, and peals of thunder. My sister and I scurried for couch pillows in which to bury our faces. Despite the terror, the glory of Oz commanded our attention.

Not since my birth had I experienced such trauma. There would be no bucket large enough for Dorothy to extinguish this foe. But then, when it seemed that all hope was gone, Dorothy's little dog, Toto, tugged on a curtain with his teeth. It opened to reveal a white-haired man standing before a control panel. Realizing that he was exposed, the wizard shouted, "Pay no attention to that man behind the curtain; the Great Oz has spoken." But lo and behold, it wasn't the Great Oz; it was merely the old man with a microphone. The charade was up, and soon Dorothy's ruby-red slippers would send her home.

I was tense. (All right, I was terrified.) Interestingly, though, as I lay in bed staring at the ceiling, my thoughts didn't concern Dorothy so much as they pondered the nature of God. My six-year-old mind superimposed the frightening attributes of the wizard upon Jesus. He was the stern judge determined to make my life miserable.

THINKING ABOUT GOD

Because I perceived Jesus to be unapproachable, I pursued other religious figures as objects of devotion. St. Christopher seemed like a natural choice, since we shared the same name. During the year of my confirmation, I had a thing for St. Patrick. (I was fascinated by his clover.) I also went through a Mary phase, seeing her as the warm mother who could help me get on speaking terms with her son. Direct interaction with Jesus was limited to the Eucharist. On more than one Sunday morning, I sat in the pew between my parents, mystified at how the same Lord who filled my nightmares could also be on my tongue in the consecrated wafer.

Have you ever taken time to sit down and reflect on what comes into your mind when you consider Jesus? It's rather amazing how many hours we can spend in church ministry without giving serious thought to the question. Since our view of Jesus Christ shapes our faith, and our faith (or lack thereof) inevitably forms our identity, we would do well to give it thought. As Tozer famously put it, "What comes into our minds when we think about God is the most important thing about us."[1]

Many of us struggle to acquire a biblically informed view of God. Our challenge is not simply seeing through a dark glass; we also have the problem of looking in the wrong direction. Therefore, as I conclude this book, the most enduring service that I can offer readers is insight into what the Bible teaches about the person of Jesus Christ.

---

1. A. W. Tozer, *The Knowledge of the Holy* (San Francisco: HarperSanFrancisco, 1961), 1.

THE TRANSFIGURATION

There are few passages in the New Testament that provide a view of the Lord Jesus quite like the passage about the transfiguration. In the three gospels where the narrative appears (Matthew, Mark, and Luke), the transfiguration is concerned with capturing a God-entranced, Jesus-focused vision. We will look at Matthew's account, which is located in chapter 17:1–8.

First, some background. After the great messianic confession of Peter in 16:16, Jesus revealed the direction of his ministry. It says, "From that time Jesus began to show his disciples that he must go to Jerusalem and suffer many things from the elders and chief priests and scribes, and be killed, and on the third day be raised" (Matt. 16:21 ESV).

In response to Jesus' statement, the disciples were outraged, so much so that "Peter took him [Jesus] aside and began to rebuke him, saying, 'Far be it from you, Lord! This shall never happen to you!'" (v. 22). Jesus then straightened Peter out: "Get behind me, Satan! You are a hindrance to me. For you are not setting your mind on the things of God, but on the things of man" (v. 23). Evidently, Peter failed to understand the person and mission of Jesus. Like Peter, we also misunderstand.

Following Peter's protest, Jesus asserts the cost of discipleship, stating that any would-be follower must deny himself, take up his cross, and follow him (Matt. 16:24).[2] This idea of embracing the rugged cross before receiving any sort of crown was presented earlier in Matthew when Satan offered Jesus the kingdoms of the world (4:8–10). Jesus resisted, understanding that suffering must precede exaltation. As for the disciples, they still didn't understand the nature of Jesus' mission.[3]

---

2. Peter's comment likely represented the thinking of all the disciples. J. D. Kingsbury, "The Figure of Peter in Matthew's Gospel as a Theological Problem," *Journal of Biblical Literature* 98 (1979): 67–83, argues along a salvation-history line that Peter was a representative figure who regularly spoke on behalf of the other disciples (Matt. 4:18–22; 8:14–15; 10:2; 14:28–31; 15:15; 16:13–20; 16:21–23).
3. Compare Matt. 4:10 with Matt. 16:23.

Matthew's gospel stresses the necessity of understanding Jesus. At stake is nothing less than one's "soul" (Matt. 16:24–26).[4] To drive home the point, certain disciples are given a glimpse of what it will look like when the Son of Man comes in glory. So chapter 16 ends and the transfiguration begins.

Following is the text from Matthew's account of the transfiguration (Matt. 17:1–8):

> After six days Jesus took with him Peter, James, and John the brother of James, and led them up a high mountain by themselves. There he was transfigured before them. His face shone like the sun, and his clothes became as white as the light. Just then there appeared before them Moses and Elijah, talking with Jesus. Peter said to Jesus, "Lord, it is good for us to be here. If you wish, I will put up three shelters—one for you, one for Moses and one for Elijah." While he was still speaking, a bright cloud enveloped them, and a voice from the cloud said, "This is my Son, whom I love; with him I am well pleased. Listen to him!" When the disciples heard this, they fell facedown to the ground, terrified. But Jesus came and touched them. "Get up," he said. "Don't be afraid." When they looked up, they saw no one except Jesus.

JESUS COMES TO FULFILL THE ANCIENT PROMISES OF ISRAEL (MATT. 17:1–3)

Sometimes we overlook the fact that Christian salvation is rooted in God's old covenant people, Israel. Ours is the faith of Abraham, Isaac, Jacob, David, and Isaiah. The historical foundation of this faith goes to the beginning of creation and steadily unfolds into the person of Jesus of Nazareth. The development of this history contains redemptive promises that are proclaimed in the garden of Eden, echo through

4. In Matthew, *psuche* (soul) frequently has an eschatological orientation, and thus may be understood as a metaphorical analogy to the Messiah's kingdom (Matt. 10:28, 39; 20:28).

time, and eventually reverberate with symphonic beauty in Christ's kingdom.

The opening of the passage is like a neon arrow pointing backward to Israel's salvation. It begins with a couple of key parallels.

For starters, notice the temporal reference "after six days":

Exod. 24:16	"And the glory of the LORD settled on Mount Sinai. For six days the cloud covered the mountain."	Matt. 17:1	"After six days Jesus took with him ... up a high mountain."

Second, like Moses, Jesus brought along three companions:

Exod. 24:9	"Moses and Aaron, Nadab and Abihu" ascended the mountain.	Matt. 17:1	"Jesus took with him Peter, James, and John the brother of James, and led them up a high mountain."

After hiking up the mountain, the Lord is transfigured, which causes his face and clothing to emanate light.[5] When we open our Old Testaments looking for examples of shining faces, it's not long before we encounter Moses. After Moses met with God atop Mount Sinai, Moses' face shone with heavenly splendor (Exod. 34:29–35; see also 2 Cor. 3:13ff.). Some years later, this same glory was applied to the hope of the nation, particularly in terms of luminescent garments. For example, looking forward to Israel's restoration from bondage, it says in Isaiah 52:1: "Awake, awake, O Zion, clothe yourself with strength.

5. The word *metamorphoo* (transfigured) occurs four times in the New Testament (Matt. 17:2; Mark 9:2; Rom. 12:2; 2 Cor. 3:18). It designates either a change of one's inmost being (Rom. 12:2; 2 Cor. 3:18) or external appearance (Matt. 17:2; Mark 9:2; compare with Exod. 34:29).

Put on your garments of splendor, O Jerusalem, the holy city. The uncircumcised and defiled will not enter you again."[6]

The transfiguration then introduces two key figures from Israel's history in Matthew 17:3, Moses and Elijah. The question of why these particular men appear to speak with Jesus is one of the most perplexing parts of the text. Five reasons have been given; the last two seem most plausible:

1. They both had unique conclusions to their time on earth (Deut. 34:1–8; 2 Kings 1:1–12).
2. They were both great miracle workers.
3. They both experienced a theophany (appearance of God) in association with Mount Sinai.
4. They are both mentioned in Malachi 4 in connection with the end times.
5. Moses represents the Law and Elijah represents the Prophets.[7]

Two questions are often raised from this verse: how were Moses and Elijah identified, and what was the topic of their discussion? There doesn't seem to be a definitive answer to the first question. (I doubt they were wearing name tags.) In regard to the second, Luke's gospel provides insight into the topic of their conversation. It says in Luke 9:30–31, "Two men, Moses and Elijah, appeared in glorious splendor, talking with Jesus. They spoke about his *departure*, which he was about to bring to fulfillment at Jerusalem" (emphasis added). The word translated "departure" is actually the Greek word *exodos*. It's perfectly acceptable to translate *exodos* as "departure." However, in this context, where Matthew is heaping up references to Israel's redemption, it's more likely that the word *exodos* refers to the deliverance of God's people through the Red Sea. A helpful summary is provided by Jerome Murphy-O'Connor, who writes, "[Moses and Eli-

6. Reference to the nation's corporate inheritance in Isa. 52:1 (in terms of "Zion" and "Jerusalem") is properly fulfilled in the singular person of Jesus Christ, according to the New Testament (Gal. 3:16; Heb. 12:22–24) and by extension his body, the church.

7. It also reflects the order of the Torah and *Neviim* of the Tanach.

jah told Jesus that his] execution would not be the end of everything, but a saving event whose role in God's plan would parallel that of the exodus from Egypt."[8] Through his imminent death and resurrection, Jesus would accomplish the ultimate exodus from sin and death on behalf of God's people.

Among the various lessons we learn from Matthew 17:1–3, I'd like to highlight a few. First, Christian faith spans the ages and thus presents an overarching narrative to life. The few years of our existence are played out on the stage of history as a brief act against the backdrop of God's masterful drama. The play is not about us; it's about *God*. He gives us the privilege of playing a part. But let us never forget, God is the director, producer, hero — the one who makes it all happen.

The Old Testament presents vivid illustrations of what it looks like to walk with God (and also what it looks like to be under his condemnation). We desperately need these lessons. In fact, they were written for this purpose, to help us live faithfully before the Lord, as it says in Romans 15:4, "For everything that was written in the past was written to teach us, so that through endurance and the encouragement of the Scriptures we might have hope."[9]

Our passage also teaches us that God faithfully fulfills his promises. Many years had passed since God spoke about redemption to Adam, Abraham, David, and other prophets. Centuries of waiting, wondering, and questioning came and went, and then, the glory of Yahweh's promise was observed on the face of his Son, Jesus. This is the character of God. His timing is notoriously different than ours, but he's always faithful.

JESUS AND HIS WORD ARE SUPREME OVER CREATION (MATT. 17:4–5)

The second most perplexing question about the transfiguration concerns the response of Peter when he offered to make three tents, one for Jesus, one for Moses, and one for Elijah. What was he thinking?

8. Jerome Murphy-O'Connor, "What Really Happened at the Transfiguration?" *Bible Review* 3 (1987): 10.

9. Also see 1 Cor. 10:6, 11.

Given the particular persons and images before him, Peter had good reason to believe it was the dawning of the messianic age.[10] He might have offered to make the tents in an attempt to retain Moses and Elijah or in some way prolong the experience. No one can say for sure, especially when Mark's gospel says of Peter's comment that "he did not know what to say, they were frightened." What we can safely say is that God disapproved. The opening phrase of verse 5 ("while he was still speaking") indicates that God's statement interrupted Peter before his suggestion was complete, at which point Peter was reproved a second time: "This is my Son, whom I love; with him I am well pleased. Listen to him!"[11]

Why did God interrupt Peter's offer? Two reasons rise to the surface. First, Peter's view of salvation was so dominated by Jewish tradition that he didn't have ears to hear Jesus. This is exposed in the preceding context, where Peter and the disciples fell under the sway of the teaching of the Pharisees and Sadducees (Matt. 16:12). Such teaching was flawed on a few levels, but especially in its reliance on human tradition over Scripture. Perhaps the most forceful place where the Lord reveals this problem is chapter 23, where he calls out the Jewish leaders for their hypocrisy. These men enjoyed being called Teachers of the Law, but they nullified God's teaching with their oral tradition. The following excerpt gives us a sense of Jesus' judgment:

> Woe to you, teachers of the law and Pharisees, you hypocrites! You shut the kingdom of heaven in men's faces. You yourselves do not enter, nor will you let those enter who are trying to.... Woe to you, blind guides!... Woe to you, teachers of the law and Pharisees, you hypocrites! You give a tenth of your spices—mint, dill and cummin. But you have neglected the more important matters of the law—justice, mercy and

10. The first-century Jew likely associated Moses and Elijah with the coming of the Messiah. See Mark Adam Elliott, *The Survivors of Israel: A Reconsideration of the Theology of Pre-Christian Judaism* (Grand Rapids, MI: Eerdmans, 2000), 465.

11. Luke excludes *agapetos* (beloved) but adds *eklegomenos* (the one I've chosen), while Mark omits the entire middle block of the statement—"with whom I am well pleased."

> faithfulness. You should have practiced the latter, without neglecting the former. You blind guides! You strain out a gnat but swallow a camel. Woe to you, teachers of the law and Pharisees, you hypocrites! You clean the outside of the cup and dish, but inside they are full of greed and self-indulgence. Blind Pharisee! First clean the inside of the cup and dish, and then the outside also will be clean. Woe to you, teachers of the law and Pharisees, you hypocrites! You are like whitewashed tombs, which look beautiful on the outside but on the inside are full of dead men's bones and everything unclean.
>
> —Matthew 23:13–27

Public rituals were gravely important to Jewish leaders; unfortunately, they had forgotten about the commands of their Scriptures, things like loving God and neighbor. Extrabiblical traditions, which were intended to protect and apply God's covenant, became so central that they practically usurped it. Jesus had no tolerance for this. With enormous passion, he denounced the scribes and Pharisees for elevating human regulations over divine revelation.

The second reason follows naturally from the first. God corrected Peter because he wasn't listening to Jesus. The Lord had explained in so many words "that he must go to Jerusalem and suffer many things at the hands of the elders, chief priests and teachers of the law, and that he must be killed and on the third day be raised to life" (Matt. 16:21), but Peter would have nothing of it (16:22). The idea of a crucified Savior was unacceptable. God's anointed deliverer was expected to come in the manner of Joshua or David—a victorious warrior who overthrows God's enemies (the Romans) and establishes everlasting peace.[12] In offering to make three tents, Peter expressed his hope that

---

12. A salient dimension of Israel's hope included liberation from oppression. Because many Jews regarded themselves to still be in a form of exile (Dan. 9:8–16; Ezra 9:7–9; Neh. 9:30–37), Israel longed for the day when God would provide liberation from her enemies (Gen. 49:1, 8–12; Num. 24:14–19; Isa. 2:2–4; 52:7–10; Dan. 2:28–45; Zeph. 3:14–15; Acts 1:6). It was thought that this liberation would usher in an age of peace (Gen. 15:18; Deut. 30:1–10; Isa. 32:1, 18).

the new age would begin immediately, apart from a cross and a tomb. Therefore, God overshadowed the disciples in a cloud and corrected them, saying, "Listen to [Jesus]!"[13]

So what does all of this have to do with accurately understanding the identity of Jesus Christ? Let me highlight a couple of lessons that especially pertain to us former Catholics. Having been raised to view Sacred Tradition as authoritative along with Scripture, we can easily make the same mistake as Peter. Although we no longer look to Catholic rituals as we once did, we can cling to an Evangelical equivalent, some person or practice that becomes a functional equivalent to Scripture. Whatever the tradition of your church, you will surely grapple with this temptation. As I sometimes tell our people at College Church, I may be ordained to pastoral ministry, but I possess no authority apart from God's Word. The biblical text is the ultimate source of truth until Jesus returns. Therefore, everything that is said and done must be measured against the plumb line of the Bible.

We must also insist that the cross and resurrection of Jesus remain central. Indeed, this is the essence of being an Evangelical, as John Stott writes: "Evangelical Christians believe that in and through Christ crucified God substituted himself for us and bore our sins, dying in our place the death we deserved to die, in order that we might be restored to his favour and adopted into his family."[14]

While it is one thing to confess this truth, it is quite another to live it out. In honest moments, we have to admit that we don't immediately jump up and down with excitement when we think about carrying our cross. The cross of Christ means suffering and pain. Anyone who blithely promotes bearing it is either a masochist or out of touch with reality. You don't need to experience a great deal of suffering to know that pain is not fun, which is why it's called pain. Rooms with padded walls are constructed for people who think otherwise.

13. This appears to be an allusion to the prophet who would be greater than Moses (Deut. 18:15; compare with Acts 3:22–23; 7:37).

14. John Stott, *The Cross of Christ* (Downers Grove, IL: InterVarsity, 1986), 7.

When I was in seminary I was teaching through Matthew's gospel at my church. My dear wife, Angela, who was pregnant at the time, sat in the front listening to my lesson. In one of my classes I had been introduced to a concept which theologians call the "upsilon vector."[15] Simply put, the vector traces the trajectory of Jesus' life in terms of his descent into apparent defeat (dying on the cross) before ascending three days later in consummate victory (in the resurrection).

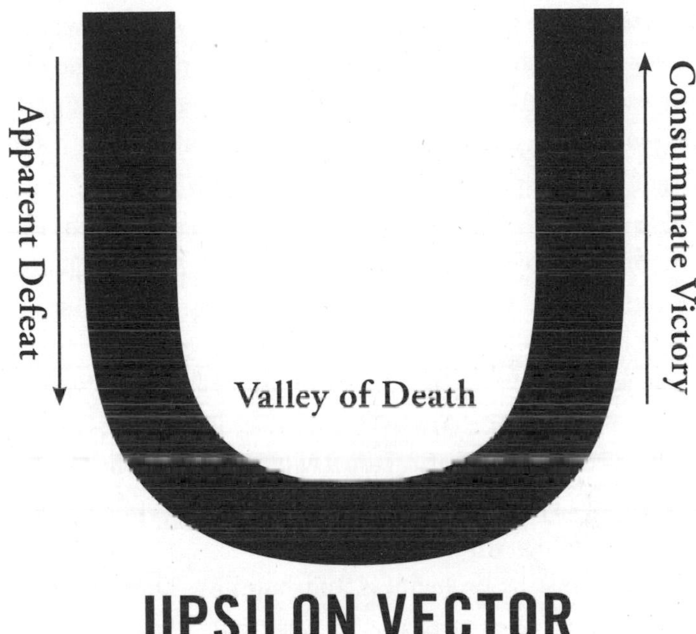

UPSILON VECTOR

The upsilon vector is a wonderful theological truth, and I preached it with great zeal. However, at one point I looked at Angela's robust belly and a question crossed my mind: what if this child introduces suffering into my life? Will I apply the truth I am now proclaiming? I swallowed hard and kept on teaching.

Two months later our first child was born. It was a boy. After being circumcised, his site continued to bleed. It was shortly thereafter

15. Dr. Royce Gruenler is the scholar whom I recall first using the term *upsilon vector*.

we learned of his condition, called severe hemophilia. You can imagine what I thought of first—the upsilon vector. Now was my opportunity to apply it. It immediately became apparent, however, that the manner in which one descends into brokenness is not with confidence and strength. It's with many tears, sleepless nights, and even depression. In Jesus' words, "My soul is overwhelmed with sorrow to the point of death" (Matt. 26:38).

Some Christians would say that God doesn't want us to have sickness and disease. We must claim healing, which is what God desires for us. I wish this were so, especially when I struggle to stick an intravenous needle into my son's tiny veins. But alas, it's not. The health-and-wealth gospel is fundamentally flawed because it fails to understand the cross of Jesus.[16] It fails to recognize that the cross was not only an instrument of torture on which God's Son died; it's also the pattern to which our lives must be conformed. Again, I quote from John Stott: "Every time we look at the cross Christ seems to say to us, 'I am here because of you. It is your sin I am bearing, your curse I am suffering, your debt I am paying, your death I am dying.' Nothing in history or in the universe cuts us down to size like the cross. All of us have inflated views of ourselves, especially in self-righteousness, until we have visited a place called Calvary. It is here, at the foot of the cross that we shrink to our true size."[17]

The cross instills brokenness and humility. Despite its heaviness and rough texture, we bear it by faith, patiently waiting for "the redemption of our bodies" (Rom. 8:23–25). And just when you expect to drop dead beneath its weight, God provides empowering grace. As Paul the apostle wrote to the church at Corinth:

---

16. Richard Bauckham says it well in his book *God Crucified: Monotheism and Christology in the New Testament* (Grand Rapids, MI: Eerdmans, 1998), 46, when he writes, "In other words, we must consider Jesus as the revelation of God. The profoundest points of New Testament Christology occur when the inclusion of the exalted Christ in the divine identity entails the inclusion of the crucified Christ in the divine identity, and when the Christological pattern of humiliation and exaltation is recognized as revelatory of God, indeed as the definitive revelation of who God is."

17. John Stott, *The Message of Galatians* (Downers Grove, IL: InterVarsity, 1968), 179.

> But we have this treasure in jars of clay to show that this all-surpassing power is from God and not from us. We are hard pressed on every side, but not crushed; perplexed, but not in despair; persecuted, but not abandoned; struck down, but not destroyed. We always carry around in our body the death of Jesus, so that the life of Jesus may also be revealed in our body.... Therefore we do not lose heart. Though outwardly we are wasting away, yet inwardly we are being renewed day by day. For our light and momentary troubles are achieving for us an eternal glory that far outweighs them all. So we fix our eyes not on what is seen, but on what is unseen. For what is seen is temporary, but what is unseen is eternal.
>
> —2 Corinthians 4:7–10, 16–18

Now that my son is seven years old, I can tell you without reservation that Angela and I have experienced dimensions of God's power on account of his hemophilia. This pattern of cruciform love has produced strength through weakness and joy from sorrow. In this way, our lives have been shaped and I trust that the kingdom has advanced.

Maybe you're reading this and thinking, "Yikes, that's not what I signed up for when I joined my church!" If these are your thoughts, I have a word of good news for you, and it comes from the remaining verses of the transfiguration narrative.

PERSONAL ENCOUNTER WITH JESUS (MATT. 17:6–8)

"When the disciples heard this, they fell facedown to the ground, terrified. But Jesus came and touched them. 'Get up,' he said. 'Don't be afraid.' When they looked up, they saw no one except Jesus."

Notice the disciples' position. They were facedown and terrified. This posture is typical among those confronted with the presence of God.[18] It is reminiscent of the prophet Daniel when he was visited by an angel.[19] And just as Daniel was touched and reassured by his

18. For example, Gen. 15:12; 28:17; Dan. 8:17–18; 10:9; Ezek. 1:28.

19. Dan. 10:7–9; compare with Rev. 1:17.

heavenly visitor, so Jesus extends his hand to encourage the disciples.[20] The Lord tells them, "Don't be afraid."

All the Old Testament images were now gone. Shining faces, the cloud, tent-making proposals — they vanished. The text says that the disciples "saw no one except Jesus." Then, in a most personal way, the Savior touched them. Jesus' hand invited his disciples to confront their fears and arise. Picture it: one moment Peter, James, and John were looking down at the dirt in terror; the next instant they were looking into the face of the Son of God. How's that for a view of Jesus?

This is the view that we should have. Yes, it is right to fear God. He alone is immortal and lives in unapproachable light (1 Tim. 6:16). Before his throne, angels sing "Holy, holy, holy is the Lord Almighty; the whole earth is full of his glory" (Isa. 6:3). Doorposts tremble and shake at the sound of his voice and anyone with a lick of sense falls down covering his mouth. It is not only presumption and pride to think that we can stand in his presence; it's downright silly. And yet, true as this is, the character of God is such that he condescends to us. When God appeared before Moses and proclaimed his character, he said, "[I am] the LORD, the LORD, the compassionate and gracious God, slow to anger, abounding in love and faithfulness" (Exod. 34:6). And how does God descend to us in love and compassion? He does it in his Son, as it says in John 1:14: "The Word became flesh and made his dwelling among us. We have seen his glory, the glory of the One and Only, who came from the Father, full of grace and truth." Does it blow your mind? It should. The eternal Word who shares divine glory with the Father comes from heaven to touch us with his redemptive love.

Would you allow me to share one more lesson before we conclude? God impressed this truth upon me in the Great White Mountains of New Hampshire while I was on retreat during seminary.

It was five in the morning when I decided to walk down to the lake with my Bible to see the sun rise. I'm really not that pious; it's

---

20. Dan. 8:18; 10:11 – 12.

just that one of the guys in my room snored so loudly that the walls shook and I got tired of listening to it. I walked a quarter of a mile along a dirt path to a clearing beside the lake. Standing at the water's edge, I sang, prayed, thought about the s'mores we consumed the night before, and looked at my watch a lot. For some reason it always seems to take longer for the sun to rise than you anticipate. In the meantime, I paced back and forth in the darkness reading my Bible in the moonlight.

After more than an hour, I looked up to the mountain peak before me and made an observation. Illuminating the tall pine trees was sunlight. The light hadn't yet descended to ground level, but it had started to shine up there on the mountain.

My friends, that's the good news of the gospel. The Son has risen from the dead! The light of the kingdom already shines, as Paul writes in Ephesians 5:14: "Wake up, O sleeper, rise from the dead, and Christ will shine on you."

Although it remains dark and lonely down here, the glory of heaven eventually will descend to earth. On that great day, we will see the splendor of Jesus' face, just as the disciples did.

Do we believe this?

Or maybe a better question is, Can the people who watch us each day, Catholic or otherwise, observe in us the substance of this belief?

May the answer be yes, by God's grace.

HOW THE CATHOLIC CHURCH BECAME WHAT IT IS

TRENT TO VATICAN II

THE COUNCIL OF TRENT (1545–63)

The Council of Trent, which met in three separate sessions between 1545 and 1563, convened in the mountain-encompassed city of Trento two hours from the current Austrian border. The Duomo (Cathedral) is an architectural wonder. Its facade includes an enormous rose window of radiant colors. Inside the entrance hall are stone lions supporting columns on the northern side with twisting pillars rising up to greet its Gothic dome. Under its cruciform roof one finds frescoes from the fourteenth century and relics of the local martyrs Sisinius, Marturius, and Alexander, who died around 397 AD. In the Crucifix Chapel is a wooden crucifix in front of which the council's issues were announced before subsequent sessions commenced in the church's presbytery.[1]

Of the six hundred Catholic bishops in Europe when the Council of Trent started, only thirty-one were in attendance for its opening.

1. In addition to being held at the Duomo, the Church of Santa Maria Maggiore was the site of the third session of the Council of Trent (April 1562 to December 1563).

The English were forbidden to attend and the French were discouraged from it. Therefore, Italians and Spaniards predominated. Such a meager showing hardly represented the church; nevertheless, the council convened.

Charles V had hoped to see the church enact simple reforms to show his rebel Protestant princes and barons that action was indeed being taken to address the religious breach which continued to undermine peace in their territories. Pope Paul III (1534–49), however, had bigger plans. In addition to reforming clerical abuses, the pope wanted to more critically define Catholic doctrine. He was especially concerned with the fundamental controversy between Catholics and Protestants: the issue of what constitutes the church's supreme authority. In short, "the Protestants taught the religious authority of Scripture alone. The council insisted on the supreme teaching office of the Roman Church—popes and bishops—as the essential interpreters of the Bible."[2] Pope Paul III was determined to set the Protestants straight.

The Council of Trent reestablished the seven sacraments and condemned the Protestant teaching of justification by faith alone. The directness of these positions was so sharply and forcefully pointed at Protestants that Charles V became concerned that it would undermine all hope of achieving political harmony among his rival states. Rome wasn't making concessions, which spelled trouble for the emperor, who had more than a few Lutherans in his empire.

Eventually, in 1549, Pope Paul III died. He favored as his successor Reginald Pole of England (who happened to be a close friend of Gasparo Contarini). As a *Spirituali* member himself, Pole believed in justification by faith alone and wanted to see it woven into the fabric of Catholic theology. Inquisitor Cardinal Gian Pietro Carafa of Naples, however, worked hard to depict Pole as a Protestant-sympathizing heretic, after which the English cardinal missed selection to the papacy by one vote. Instead, Julius III was given the papal crown on the condition that he would actively support the work of

2. Bruce Shelley, *Church History in Plain Language*, 2nd ed. (Dallas: Word, 1995), 277.

Trent.[3] Pole was urged to leave the council (allegedly on account of a nervous breakdown) when his position concerning faith was about to be condemned.

Under Pope Julius III (1550–55) the Council of Trent continued to focus on the business of condemning Protestants. In particular, delegates emphasized the Catholic understanding of Eucharist—that the bread and wine turn entirely into the physical body and blood of Christ. Following the papacy of Julius III, inquisitor Cardinal Gian Pietro Carafa became Pope Paul IV (1555–59). He refused to reconvene the council as a protest against what he considered its independent spirit. Nevertheless, by taking control of the Jesuits and by enforcing a host of new religious rules, he was effective in pounding the wedge more deeply between Protestants and Rome.

The final pope to preside over the council was Pius IV (1559–65).[4] Like his predecessors, he further emphasized Roman Catholic authority over the Protestant position of Scripture alone. When the Council of Trent drew to a close, he sealed it with the bull *Injunctum nobis*, which included a doctrinal statement required of all Catholics.[5] The document highlights the anti-Protestant impulse of the council: "I recognize the Holy Catholic and Apostolic *Roman* Church [emphasis added] as the mother and mistress of all churches; and I vow and swear true obedience to the Roman Pontiff, the successor of blessed Peter, the chief of the Apostles and the vicar of Jesus Christ."[6]

Whether Trent constituted a "Counter" or a "Catholic" Reformation is a matter of dispute. It was probably both. The official dogmas formulated in her sessions boldly countered and condemned Protestant theology; however, at the same time, positive reforms also

---

3. Stephen Tomkins, *A Short History of Christianity* (Grand Rapids, MI: Eerdmans, 2005), 155.
4. Although the popes didn't actually attend the council in person, their voices were mediated through key cardinals.
5. It was called the "Form for Profession of the Orthodox Catholic Faith" (also referred to as the "Creed of Pius IV").
6. Martin Marty, *A Short History of Christianity*, 2nd ed. (Philadelphia: Fortress, 1987), 202.

were instituted to curb clerical abuses and promote spiritual renewal. Whichever of these emphases one might prefer, we can all agree that at the Council of Trent, the Roman Catholic Church clarified for everyone her beliefs and practices. She was "the Holy, Catholic, and Apostolic Roman Church." Behind the thick walls of Trent's cathedral, Rome built for herself a fortress in which there was only one papal throne. Catholic historian Joseph Lortz summarizes the legacy of Trent, writing, "[T]his became the most papal of all councils, a veritable precursor of Vatican I, and without which Vatican I could never have been conceived at all."[7] To this council we now turn.

VATICAN I (1869–70)

Three hundred years later, on July 18, 1870, there was a severe thunderstorm in Rome. As Pope Pius IX stood in St. Peter's Basilica, his voice was hardly audible over the stormy claps and rumbles which sounded off the ceiling. Despite some extra candles brought to his lectern, the pope struggled to read the text before him. Bishops strained to capture his words. Assuming they sat close enough to his lectern, they heard him say the following: "If any one, therefore, shall say that blessed Peter the apostle was not appointed the prince of all the apostles and the visible head of the whole church militant; or that the same directly and immediately received from the same our Lord Jesus Christ a primacy of honor only, and not of true and proper jurisdiction: let him be anathema [cursed]."[8]

The emphasis of Pius IX was in many ways a continuation (and climax) of what started at the Council of Trent. Even though three centuries separate the events, they are closely connected in the vein of papal authority. To understand the nature of this relationship, we must step back from Vatican I to consider the history which preceded it.

---

7. Joseph Lortz, *The Reformation in Germany*, vol. 2, trans. Ronald Walls (New York: Herder and Herder, 1968), 238.

8. Philip Schaff, *The Creeds of Christendom* (New York: Harper and Row, 1931; repr., Grand Rapids, MI: Baker, 1998), 259–60. Citations are to the Baker edition.

In the year 1789, when the French Revolution began, the Roman Catholic Church still reigned over the structures of Western Europe. From inside her religious fortress, it appeared that life was proceeding normally. However, the traditional order would soon be turned on its head.

Like most revolutions, the Age of Enlightenment started in the realm of ideas and words, but it wasn't long before discussion turned to action. On July 14, 1789, when the Parisian mob stormed the city of Bastille, the cat was out of the bag. This European feline wasn't the kind of friendly pet that sits on your lap; it was a lion. Because the Church of Rome was a standard menu item of the old, established order, it became a prominent part of the lion's diet. For example, in the 1790s one of these revolutionary groups called the National Assembly endeavored to reform the church. However, when the assembly undercut control of the pope in France and required church office-holders to do the same, the church divided down the middle. Clergy in virtually every town and village throughout France locked horns. Eventually, the revolutionary leaders drove more than thirty thousand priests from their native towns into hiding.[9]

With each passing year, the revolutionary lion grew larger and fiercer, especially in France. After Louis XVI let in a foreign invasion to address his radicals, rioting peasants showed him the door. Actually, they sent him and his family to the guillotine. As heads were rolling, the new parliament abolished Christianity in exchange for the humanist ideology of Voltaire and Rousseau. Reason was worshiped as God, the religious calendar was replaced by ten-day weeks, and saints' days became holidays celebrating fruit, vegetables, and flowers. (Yes, I was also surprised to learn that the original flower children were French.) However, in 1799, just ten years after the French Revolution started, a man drove a sword through the heart of the modernist lion. His name was Napoleon Bonaparte.

---

9. Shelley, *Church History*, 357.

Under Napoleon's leadership, the French army conquered Italy, including the city of Rome. Although the primary object of his worship was himself, Napoleon recognized Catholicism as a friend to his social order. Historian Stephen Tomkins describes what this "friendship" looked like:

> So Napoleon offered Pope Pius VII a deal. He would restore the church if the Pope approved his regime, but bishops would be chosen by and swear allegiance to Napoleon, and Jews and Protestants would still be tolerated. Pius agreed, but he became increasingly annoyed by Napoleon's manipulation of the church. In 1804, Napoleon induced him to come and crown him emperor in Notre Dame, repaying the favour Pope Leo had paid Charlemagne 1,000 years before, but in a pointed twist of the tale, Napoleon whipped the crown out of the Pope's hands at the last minute and crowned himself.... Finally, when Napoleon annexed the Papal State to France, Pius excommunicated him, so Napoleon arrested the Pope.[10]

As the French megalomaniac was getting back at the world for all the short-little-boy jokes he was the butt of as a kid, Napoleon was unwittingly taking the revolution farther than it had gone before. He not only broke the alliance of throne and altar in France (as revolutionaries had dramatically displayed on November 10, 1793, when they desecrated the high altar of Notre Dame with the Goddess of Reason), but he inadvertently carried this division to Rome itself. Swiss and other mercenaries offered virtually no resistance to Napoleon's invasion of 1796. Humiliated by the French sword, Pope Pius VI (and his successor Pius VII) were divested of political power.

When Napoleon's empire collapsed in 1815 and he was banished to a desolate island in the Atlantic, the Congress of Vienna restored the Papal States and placed them under Austrian protection; however, the days of her self-governing power were now gone.

10. Tomkins, *A Short History*, 205.

After a few years of relative peace, a movement for Italian independence and solidarity called *Risorgimento* (rebirth) arose in Sardinia. Eager to see the Italian peninsula united under a common flag, revolutionaries considered the Papal States to be a medieval vestige which stood in the way of their dream. A host of conspiracies and revolts characterized the following decades (especially between 1831–49) as liberal factions jockeyed for power. The pontiff found himself in the middle of this explosive politick.

At first, proponents of *Risorgimento* regarded Pope Pius IX (1846–78) as an ally, but their alliance didn't last long. Historian Bruce Shelley offers a cogent summary of how things soured:

> Liberals initially welcomed Pope Pius IX. He was a warm, kindly, well-meaning man, and the liberals took him for a true reformer when, on 14 March 1848, he gave the Papal States a constitution that permitted the people a moderate degree of participation in their government. Some dreamed of an Italian federation under the pope. But Pius suddenly changed his mind about the Papal States when revolutionaries assassinated the first papal prime minister, Count Pellegrino Rossi. Revolution broke out in Rome, and Pius was forced to flee. With French military help he regained Rome and the Papal States, but this time Pius insisted to a return to the old absolutist rule.[11]

Through a series of eventful (and ironic) turns, Rome found security in the protection of French troops. But the respite was short lived. When the Franco-Prussian War drew the French military home from Italy, Rome was left unprotected. A new Italian army led by nationalists immediately attacked the Papal States, and Pope Pius IX surrendered. Following a referendum, Rome was declared Italy's capital city. When it was formally annexed on 20 October 1870, one thousand

11. Shelley, *Church History*, 359.

years of Papal State sovereignty came to an end. Consequently, Pius IX retreated into a self-imposed captivity in the Vatican.

When Victor Emmanuel, the first king of a united Italy, chose Rome as his residence in 1871, the pope was furious. He prohibited Italy's Catholics from participating in the new political establishment, including elections. This moratorium not only muted the Catholic voice in political and social affairs, it also engendered a rather strident anticlerical attitude. It wasn't until Benito Mussolini concluded the Lateran Treaty in 1929 that the church's claim on Rome was resolved. The pope was forced to renounce any right to the former Papal States. He was, however, given sovereignty in the Vatican territory.[12]

We can only imagine the pope's frustration (and humiliation) when he was forced to surrender the Papal States after the church had possessed them for more than a millennium. While we don't know what was going through his mind, his response to the situation is a matter of historical record. In 1870, the same year when political rule was seized from Pope Pius IX, he declared the doctrine of papal infallibility—that a pope is preserved from error when solemnly pronouncing teaching of faith and morals as being contained in divine revelation. Although Pius IX was stripped of his political role, he possessed a jurisdiction beyond the reach of any king or prince—the spiritual realm. In this realm there was one earthly throne and one pontiff with the authority to speak from it.[13]

The concept of papal infallibility had been considered for a few decades before it was made official. During the 1850s a Jesuit publi-

---

12. Ibid., 360.

13. The Declaration of the First Vatican Council asserts that when the pope speaks *ex cathedra* (from the chair), he does so as God's inspired spokesman. "In the discharge of his office of pastor and doctor of all Christians, he defines, in virtue of his supreme apostolic authority, a doctrine of faith or morals to be held by the universal Church, [and] is endowed by the divine assistance promised to him in blessed Peter with that infallibility with which our divine redeemer willed that the Church should be furnished in defining doctrine of faith or morals; and, therefore, that such definitions of Roman pontiff are irreformable of themselves and not in virtue of the consent of the Church" (Barry J. Colman, ed., *Readings in Church History*, vol. 3, *The Modern Era, 1789 to the Present* [Westminster: Newman, 1965], 78–79).

cation taught that God's thoughts are mediated through the papacy. "Hymns appeared addressed, not to God, but to Pius IX; and some dared to speak of the Holy Fathers as 'the vice-God of humanity.' "[14]

In 1854, the pope continued along a papal-centered trajectory by establishing the dogma of Mary's immaculate conception, the belief that Jesus' mother was conceived without original sin. Of particular interest was the way he did it. Although fifty-four cardinals and 140 bishops were present for the pronouncement, the council didn't make the decision (as was the custom); rather, the pope alone made it. This innovation foreshadowed the doctrine of papal infallibility which would be declared sixteen years later in the darkness of St. Peter's amid peals of thunder and flashes of lightning.[15] Finally, the movement toward papal supremacy that started at Trent had reached its climax.

By the conclusion of 1870, the popular image of the Roman Catholic Church was solidified. The dogmatic formulations of Trent and Vatican I had created an impregnable fortress into which the faithful fled for security from the fierce lion of modernism, which roamed free outside. This citadel image continued into the twentieth century. Roman Catholic journalist David Gibson provides a snapshot: "In a 1906 encyclical, Pius X said that the 'one duty' of the laity 'is to allow themselves to be led, and like a docile flock, to follow the Pastors.' In 1907 the American hierarchy followed suit with a similar directive: 'The Church is not a republic or a democracy, but a monarchy; ... all her authority is from above and rests in her Hierarchy ... [While] the faithful of the laity have divinely given rights to receive all the blessed ministrations of the Church, they have absolutely no right whatever to rule and govern.' "[16]

---

14. Shelley, *Church History*, 361.

15. Earle Cairns, *Christianity through the Centuries: A History of the Christian Church* (Grand Rapids, MI: Zondervan, 1981), 395. Since the 1870 solemn declaration of papal infallibility by Vatican I, this power has been used only once: in 1950, when Pius XII defined the assumption of Mary as being an article of faith for Roman Catholics.

16. David Gibson, *The Coming Catholic Church: How the Faithful Are Shaping a New American Catholicism* (San Francisco: Harper, 2003), 48.

As the century unfolded, a top-down structure was also demonstrated by the papal encyclical *Humani Generis* of 1950. In it, Pope Pius XII (1939–58) "decried the attempts of some theologians to update Church teachings and 'to weaken the significance of the dogmas ... by seeking to free them from concepts and formulations long held by the Church and to return *instead to the language of the Bible* and the Fathers.'"[17] Yet within just twelve years, a pontiff arose who loved fresh air and had an uncanny ability to charm lions.

VATICAN II (1962–65)

"There are two books you must read if you want to study Vatican II (after the council's documents): *History of Vatican II,* five volumes edited by Giuseppe Alberigo, and *Modern Catholicism: Vatican II and After,* edited by Adrian Hastings." This is what my professor friend told me. When I finally mustered enough courage to pick these dense tomes off the library bookshelf, I found a table and opened Alberigo's first volume expecting to have the most boring afternoon of my life. After reading a few chapters, I looked up at the clock and discovered to my surprise that two hours had passed. It was then I realized that the story of Vatican II is, in fact, a scintillating drama.

Cardinal Angelo Roncalli of Venice (1881–1963) came from a humble background. He was widely regarded as a "pastor's pastor," a lover of people. After his election to the papacy on October 28, 1958, at the ripe age of seventy-seven, he took the name John XXIII (based on his father's name and his reading of chapter 10 of John's gospel). On that same day, he summarized the personal aims of his pontificate in terms of emulating Jesus, the Good Shepherd. Few people would have suspected that this warm old man in the twilight of life would be responsible for calling one of the most significant councils in the history of the church: Vatican II.[18]

---

17. Shelley, *Church History*, 451, emphasis added.
18. I highly recommend Thomas Cahill's biography *Pope John XXIII: A Life* (New York: Penguin, 2008).

Pope John XXIII (1958–63) enjoyed making new friends and was especially sympathetic to the marginalized and suffering. He often ventured out to visit orphanages and jails, and when a group of Jews once visited him, he embraced them with the biblical greeting, "I am Joseph, your brother." He even granted a papal audience to a traveling circus and fondly patted a lion cub named Dolly.[19] The world soon learned that this pontiff was not only calm among lions but also impervious to the roar of modernity which had sent his predecessors running defensively into the Vatican fortress.

Instead of the citadel image of the Roman church that was forged during the age of Pius IX, Vatican II portrayed the church as a pilgrim people on the move throughout the modern world.[20] Toward this end, the council was designed to pursue "pastoral" aims (unlike Trent and Vatican I, which focused mainly on doctrinal reform).[21] The particular term used by John XXIII for this pursuit was *aggiornamento*, an Italian word meaning "bringing up to date." Among its chief concerns was the question of where church authority resides and how such authority should be expressed on the parish level. Would the song of the Lamb ring out from the clerical citadel, or would it proceed from the lips of Catholic parishioners?

On Thursday, October 11, 1962, Vatican II started with the continuous procession of bishops in miters and flowing vestments entering St. Peter's Basilica. After the 2,400 council fathers were in place, the portable throne of Pope John XXIII was lowered at the entrance, whereupon he proceeded to walk down the 624-foot aisle amid clerical cheers and applause. Pope John XXIII expressed hope that if he

---

19. Ibid., 452–53.

20. In its own words, "Christ summons the Church to continual reformation as she sojourns here on earth. The Church is always in need of this, insofar as she is an institution of men here on earth. Thus if, in various times and circumstances, there have been deficiencies in moral conduct or in church discipline, or even in the way that church teaching has been formulated—to be carefully distinguished from the deposit of faith itself—these can and should be set right at the opportune moment" (Decree on Ecumenism 6).

21. In the words of Pope John XXIII, the council would be "predominantly pastoral in character" (Ralph M. Wiltgen, *The Rhine Flows into the Tiber* [Devon: Augustine, 1978], 15).

were not still alive by the council's end, he would have the privilege of watching its conclusion from heaven. This statement turned out to be more prophetic than anyone realized. On June 3, 1963, after completing the first of four sessions, Pope John XXIII died.

The general sessions of Vatican II were held in the autumns of four successive years from 1962 through 1965. Given the lively debate that characterized session one, some questioned whether the council would resume. But it did. Pope Paul VI, the successor of John XXIII, convened the second session on September 29, 1963.

Space won't permit a thorough examination of the Vatican II drama, even though the story is well worth telling. Our main concern is to consider how the distinctive threads of church authority were woven together. To gain perspective on the tapestry's finished form, we will consider a couple of anecdotes. The first occurred during the council; the second happened just after it.

Generally speaking there were two extremes represented at the council. "Some Catholic conservatives hoped to reassert the kind of top-down papal supremacy that had characterized the decrees of the First Vatican Council of 1869–70."[22] The Roman Curia (the Vatican's senior level governing body) championed this position. "[On the other side of the spectrum were radicals who] wanted the church to embrace progressive movements of social renewal and theological modernism."[23] The clash of these factions produced more than a few sparks.

The question of whether it was appropriate for the Mass to be spoken in the vernacular instead of Latin provoked an especially fierce debate. An outspoken voice was Archbishop Enrico Dante, who served as the Secretary of the Sacred Congregation. As a Curia member (and expert Latinist) he insisted that "Latin should continue to be the language of the liturgy, and the vernacular should be used only for instructions and certain prayers."[24]

22. Mark Noll, *Turning Points: Decisive Moments in the History of Christianity* (Grand Rapids, MI: Baker: 2001), 302.

23. Ibid., 302.

24. Wiltgen, *The Rhine*, 28.

The liturgy debate continued for quite some time. Eventually, the most powerful Curia member of all, Cardinal Alfredo Ottaviani, took the podium to exhort progressives on how they should consider the Mass (or so he thought). The story is told by Catholic historian Ralph M. Wiltgen:

> On October 30, the day after his seventy-second birthday, Cardinal Ottaviani addressed the council to protest against the drastic changes which were being suggested in the Mass. "Are we seeking to stir up wonder, or perhaps scandal, among the Christian people, by introducing changes in so venerable a rite, that has been approved for so many centuries and is now so familiar? The rite of Holy Mass should not be treated as if it were a piece of cloth to be refashioned according to the whim of each generation." Speaking without a text, because of his partial blindness, he exceeded the ten-minute time limit which all had been requested to observe. Cardinal Tisserant, Dean of the Council Presidents, showed his watch to Cardinal Alfrink, who was presiding that morning. When Cardinal Ottaviani reached fifteen minutes, Cardinal Alfrink rang the warning bell. But the speaker was so engrossed in his topic that he did not notice the bell, or purposely ignored it. At a signal from Cardinal Alfrink, a technician switched off the microphone. After confirming the fact by tapping the instrument, Cardinal Ottaviani stumbled back to his seat in humiliation. The most powerful cardinal in the Roman Curia had been silenced, and the Council Fathers clapped with glee.[25]

This anecdote epitomizes the daring spirit of Vatican II and is one of many examples of how the tide of religious authority turned during the council. Contrary to the fortress mentality, the church reached out to the world in fresh ways. For instance, Protestants, who were

25. Ibid., 28–29.

previously considered to be damned heretics (since the Council of Trent), were elevated to the more favorable plane of "separated brethren." Some of them were even invited to observe the council. Ecumenical bridges were also built to Eastern Orthodoxy and Judaism. The sharp wedge between tradition and Scripture was removed.[26] A decree on the freedom of religion was declared which permanently eliminated inquisitions and other techniques of religious coercion. Papal authority was diffused as the role of bishops was stepped up. Bible study was encouraged for lay Catholics along with more emphasis on personal faith. Perhaps the most obvious reform came in the liturgy itself. Professor David Wells describes the change:

> Formerly, worship had tended to be mechanical, external, carried on by a priest who was almost oblivious to the people in the Church. They tended to be merely spectators at an event essentially external to them. [The council document titled] *Mediator Dei* sought to reverse this, arguing that the faithful are not "mute onlookers" but should share in the worship service with the priest. The encyclical even allowed that the laity has a priestly function to fulfill. While falling short of endorsing a full doctrine of the priesthood of all believers, the encyclical went a long way toward reversing a suffocating clericalism under which Catholicism had suffered and toward endorsing the need for subjective involvement in Christian faith.[27]

In regard to religious authority, Wells points out a critical issue with the words "subjective involvement." The idea is so fundamental to Protestant belief and practice that Evangelicals easily overlook the

26. Scripture *and* tradition, asserted Trent (Session 4.8; 8 April 1546), were to be embraced as two equally authoritative sources of divine revelation. At Vatican II, four hundred years later, Rome emphasized that Scripture and tradition flow from the same divine wellspring, merge into a unity, and move toward the same goal (*Dogmatic Constitution on Divine Revelation* 9, 18 November 1865; see also *Catechism of the Catholic Church*, 2nd ed., para. 80).

27. David F. Wells, *Revolution in Rome* (Downers Grove, IL: InterVarsity, 1972), 11–12.

profound step that it represented. For lay Catholics, however, the shift was drastic enough to take one's breath away. No longer was worship and outreach limited to the ordained clergy; all Catholics were now invited to participate. Historian Bruce Shelley explains part of the effect: "Until the arrival of Pope John and the Second Vatican Council, the typical Catholic took the authoritarian structure of the Church as a dictate of divine revelation. They thought of the pope as a kind of superhuman ruler whose every word was a command invested with supernatural authority; even the bishop they regarded with awe. In this state of affairs, few Catholics questioned the autocratic procedure customary in the Church, though to outsiders they often appeared medieval. No one dared to challenge the bishop in the rule of his diocese as a personal fief, or the pastor running his parish."[28]

A helpful way to appreciate the revolutionizing effect of Rome's having shifted religious authority from the ordained clergy to its laypeople is by considering the change in Catholic music during the twentieth century. Because songs effectively communicate one's values and priorities like few other media, they provide a fascinating window into the time period. An excellent example is a hymn titled "Long Live the Pope" by Right Reverend Monsignor Hugh Henry. It is believed that Henry wrote the song in 1908, and thereafter it appeared in the famed St. Gregory Hymnal, which was the most popular Catholic choir hymnal in the United States from the 1920s until the 1960s. The song is representative of Catholic faith before Vatican II. Even if you're not a professional hymnologist, you're likely to see its emphasis.

Long live the Pope!
His praises sound
Again and yet again:
His rule is over space and time:
His throne the heart of men:
All hail! The Shepherd Pope of Rome,
The theme of loving song:

28. Shelley, *Church History*, 458.

Let all the earth his glory sing
And heav'n the strain prolong.
Beleaguered by the foes of earth,

Beset by hosts of hell,
He guards the loyal flock of Christ,
A watchful sentinel:
And yet, amid the din and strife,
The clash of mace and sword,
He bears alone the Shepherd Staff,
The champion of the Lord.
His signet is the Fisherman's

No sceptre does he bear
In meek and lowly majesty
He rules from Peter's chair
And yet from every tribe and tongue
From every clime and zone
Three hundred million voices sing
The glory of his throne.[29]
Then raise the chant,

With heart and voice,
In Church and school and home:
"Long live the Shepherd of the Flock!
Long live the Pope of Rome!"
Almighty Father bless his work,
Protect him in his ways,
Receive his prayer, fulfill his hopes,
And grant him length of days!

If you come from a Catholic background and you're under the age of fifty, I'd like to ask you a question. Have you ever sung this song? If

---

29. For some reason this third stanza is omitted from the WETN website: *www.ewtn.com/jp2/papal3/long_live.htm*.

you answered yes, you are part of a *very* small minority. On the other hand, if you were raised in Catholic America between 1920 and 1960, it might have been as popular for you as Luther's "A Mighty Fortress" is for Protestants. Simply put, since the conclusion of Vatican II in 1965, there's been a marked decrease in the number of hymns that exalt the glory of "Peter's chair." Conversely, there have been many more songs written about the Catholic individual's heart of devotion to God. This change of emphasis has modified, to one degree or another, the profile of virtually every Catholic parish on the face of the earth. Such modification continues to unfold today and promises to do so into the future, as Professor Wells points out: "The pivot on which the future turns would seem to be the shift towards subjective religious experience and away from objective Church allegiance. This emphasis will mean that two men may regard each other as Catholics, not because both adhere to the same (objective) teaching but because both appear to share the same (subjective) experience. In an existential age, *how* you believe is far more important than *what* you believe."[30]

On account of the council's movement toward personal experience, some contend that the modern Roman Catholic Church is now practically synonymous with Protestantism. A friend of mine recently made this argument. In doing so, he put forth Martin Luther as the poster boy whose *personal* conscience was captive to God's Word. "This is now the Catholic position," he contended.

I can understand why one would reach my friend's conclusion. Unfortunately, the correlation between the Protestant Reformation and Vatican II essentially is flawed. It fails to recognize that an emphasis on personal faith was only one of several threads woven into the Second Vatican tapestry. The strand called "papal supremacy" was also entwined. To understand the significance of this papal thread, we will consider an event that transpired just three years after the council — the encyclical called *Humanae vitae*.

30. Wells, *Revolution in Rome*, 118.

The decade after Vatican II was among the most turbulent in the modern history of Catholicism. With authoritarian structures held in contempt and democratic reforms promoted left and right, renewal seemed to be omnipresent. Shelley describes these years, writing, "So many spiritual and religious landmarks were suddenly swept away that the average Catholic was left in a state of complete bewilderment."[31]

The church's bewilderment is examined by Professor Ralph M. McInerny of Notre Dame in his book *What Went Wrong with Vatican II.* He provides an assessment of what happened in 1968 when Pope Paul VI issued his infamous encyclical *Humanae vitae*, which condemned the use of artificial methods of contraception.[32] The encyclical ignited a political inferno. During the days after the pope's announcement, untold numbers of Catholics left the church.[33] At the risk of pressing the lion and fortress metaphor too far, the fallout was akin to the Siegfried and Roy catastrophe of 2003, when a Las Vegas audience observed Roy getting mauled by the large cat. A lot of discomfort and consternation followed.

Pope Paul VI was courageous; we must give him that. Jumping into the lion's cage with a chair and whip might be less daunting than the opposition he faced. In his decision, the pontiff moved against the overwhelming consensus shared by his Birth Control Commission, bishops, clergy, and laypeople.[34] Professor McInerny describes the fireworks set off by the pope's decision:

---

31. Shelley, *Church History*, 457.

32. Catholic theology maintains that God created sexual intercourse to be unitive and procreative. Therefore, the church considers deliberate altering of fertility with the intention of preventing procreation to be sinful. However, certain Natural Family Planning (NFP) methods, such as the "rhythm method," are approved by the church.

33. "Amid all the upheaval, the Church experienced a major exodus of priests, brothers, and nuns. From 1962 to 1974 the total number of seminarians in the United States alone decreased by 31 percent; and between 1966 and 1972 nearly 8,000 American priests left the public ministry" (Shelley, *Church History*, 459).

34. Some bishops were evidently so certain that Pope Paul VI would approve the use of artificial contraception that they granted permission for birth control to parishioners before the encyclical was pronounced. For instance, "The Archdiocese of Munich had, some time before, issued official instructions to priests that a Catholic couple who, 'under their mutual Christian responsibility, seeking the true welfare of the child, come to believe that they cannot avoid a contraceptive conduct, must not be rashly accused of abusing marriage.' Now even Cardinal Doepfner, Archbishop of Munich, was in a rather difficult

Throughout July 29, the very day Pope Paul VI's encyclical was made public, it became clear that *Humanae Vitae* was encountering massive clerical resistance. It was being treated with scorn and contempt everywhere. Long before they could have read the encyclical, Catholic theologians, sociologists, and journalists were dissociating themselves from its reported teaching. Said Fr. Robert Johann, S.J., to the *New York Times*, "The hope, I think, is that educated Catholics will ignore this document."[35]

Father Charles Curran, associate professor of theology at the Catholic University of America and vice president of the American Theological Society, spearheaded an effort to solicit signatures for a statement to be published about the encyclical. When the statement was first issued, there were eighty-seven signatures. The number of those wishing to associate themselves with Father Curran's refusal to accept *Humanae Vitae* was to swell in subsequent days to more than two hundred.[36]

The two hundred signatures were published in the *New York Times* on July 30, 1968, below several of Father Curran's protests. Following are a few of his statements:

> It is common teaching in the Church that Catholics may dissent from authoritative, non-infallible teachings of the Magisterium, when sufficient reasons for doing so exist.[37]

---

position" (Ralph M. McInerny, *What Went Wrong with Vatican II: The Catholic Crisis* [Manchester: Sophia Institute, 1998], 54–55).

35. Ibid., 59–60.

36. Ibid., 60.

37. Ibid., 64. This statement is misleading. The Vatican II document titled *Lumen gentium* affirms the binding authority of papal encyclicals when it says, "This religious submission of mind and will must be shown in a special way to the authentic magisterium of the Roman Pontiff, even when he is not speaking *ex cathedra*; that is, it must be shown in such a way that his supreme magisterium is acknowledged with reverence, the judgments made by him are sincerely adhered to, according to his manifest mind and will. His mind and will in the matter may be known either from the character of the documents, from his frequent repetition of the same doctrine, or from his manner of speaking" (*Lumen gentium*, no. 25).

> Therefore, as Roman Catholic theologians, conscious of our duty and our limitations, we conclude that spouses may responsibly decide according to their *conscience* that artificial contraception in some circumstances is permissible and indeed necessary to preserve and foster the values and sacredness of marriage.[38]

> It is our conviction also that true commitment to the mystery of Christ and the Church requires a candid statement of mind at this time by all Catholic theologians.[39]

Please note Father Curran's use of the word "conscience" and the need for "a candid statement of mind." This is the personal faith emphasis of Vatican II (and more than a little Martin Luther, for that matter). On this basis, it has been common since 1968 for Catholics to argue against *Humanae vitae* by citing the statement of journalist H. L. Menchen, who said, "It is now quite lawful for a Catholic woman to avoid pregnancy by a resort to mathematics, though she is still forbidden to resort to physics and chemistry."[40] What we must realize is that *the very existence* of this argument was made possible by Vatican II, which, unlike in previous years, provided the space and relative freedom to express it.[41]

After citing the Reverend Charles Curran's article in his book, McInerny offers a summary of its significance. This is the punch line: "And yet, despite its haste and Olympian condescension, this statement makes clear that the actual content of *Humanae Vitae* was of secondary importance to the signers of the statement. Their true tar-

38. McInerny, *What Went Wrong*, 64, emphasis added.

39. Ibid.

40. Tomkins, *A Short History*, 234.

41. Father Curran explicitly connects his rationale to Vatican II earlier in the *Times* article, where he writes, "[W]e take exception to the ecclesiology implied and the methodology used by Paul VI in the writing and promulgation of the document. They are incompatible with the Church's authentic self-awareness as expressed in and suggested by the acts of the Second Vatican Council" (McInerny, *What Went Wrong*, 61).

get was the papacy; the real burden of their remarks had to do with the locus of authority in the Church, indeed with the very nature of the Church."[42]

McInerny's conclusion supports our thesis. Although birth control was a massive issue, it points to the larger theological question of how Catholic authority operates in the church: to what extent can the pope dictate doctrine and how binding are such edicts upon the consciences of individual believers? The white-hot controversy continues among Catholics today.

I suppose the biggest takeaway from this section is the perspective that it offers on why the Catholic Church can at times sound so surprisingly Evangelical and at other times appear to be miles away from what we consider to be biblically grounded faith. It is the reason why, for instance, we may see Pope Benedict as such an enigma. If you read the pontiff's sermon from Yankee Stadium (the so called "Sermon on the Mound") or his book *Jesus of Nazareth*, you'll find that all in all they are wonderfully Evangelical. They're more Christ-centered and substantive than many, perhaps most, Evangelical sermons. Then there are his many insightful books exhorting the church to contend for a culture of life and standard of truth in our neopagan world. At the same time, the pope is also the author of *Dominus Iesus*, which asserts that Protestant congregations have legitimacy as churches only insofar as they derive it from the Catholic Church. How do we explain this strange mixture? Simple, it's the Vatican I and Vatican II voices speaking simultaneously. Evangelicals must accept that this combination is integral to the DNA of today's Catholic Church and shouldn't expect the tension to go away any time soon.

42. Ibid., 65.

DISCUSSION QUESTIONS

CHAPTER 1

Understanding Why Catholics Become Evangelical

1. Identify a positive memory from your Catholic background, one which served to establish or nurture your faith.
2. In the section "Confronted by Death," Chris explains how the loss of his grandfather caused him to reflect on the purpose of life. What events in your life have stimulated the same sort of questioning for you?
3. What is the fundamental difference between a Catholic and an Evangelical Protestant understanding of Church authority?[1]
   a. The Catholic view:
   b. The Evangelical view:
4. What are the main reasons you chose to leave the Catholic Church?
   a. With which of the five reasons outlined in the first half of *Holy Ground* do you resonate?
   b. In what order of priority would you put your reasons?
5. What insight have you acquired from this chapter?

Additional Reading

Galea, Ray. *Nothing in My Hand I Bring.* Australia: Matthias Media, 2007.

Geisler, Norman L., and Ralph E. MacKenzie. *Roman Catholics and Evangelicals: Agreements and Differences.* Grand Rapids, MI: Baker, 1995.

---

1. The answer boils down to our different view of how the life and authority of Jesus are embodied in his church and by extension into the world. Catholic theology sees a correlation between the person of Jesus and the church institution—the one, holy, Roman Catholic, and apostolic church. Evangelicals, on the other hand, correlate Jesus the living Word to Jesus the written Word (Scripture).

CHAPTER 2

Reason One: Full-Time Faith

1. How does the "image of God" relate to the divine purpose of humanity?
2. How do Catholics and Evangelicals differ in their understanding of how the church represents God's kingdom?
3. What is the church's divine purpose?
4. How have your personal routines of Christian worship and devotion changed since you became an Evangelical?
5. How do these routines get worked out in your ministry, in your workplace, and among your friends?
6. Dorothy Sayers asks a profound question: "How can anyone remain interested in a religion which seems to have no concern with nine-tenths of his life?" On a scale of one to ten, rate your ability to connect the dots between your Christian faith and the various tasks that you perform each week. How can you improve?
7. What insight have you acquired from this chapter?

Additional Reading

Banks, Robert. *Redeeming the Routines: Bringing Theology to Life.* Grand Rapids, MI: Baker, 1993.

CHAPTER 3

A Portrait of Evangelical Faith: Martin Luther

1. Historian Martin Marty describes Martin Luther as a "wrestler with God, indeed, as a God-obsessed seeker of certainty and assurance."[2] How do you relate to Luther's experience?
2. How was Luther's ministry similar to that of John Wycliffe (1324–84) and John Hus (c. 1369–1415)?
3. Where do you see Luther's questions and concerns expressed today, perhaps even in your own experience?

2. Martin Marty, *Martin Luther* (New York: Viking Penguin, 2004), xii.

4. What do you think about the argument which some make that since the reforms of Vatican II, Catholics and Protestants are essentially the same?
5. How would you summarize the teaching of *sola Scriptura* (Scripture alone) and of what importance does it have to your faith?
6. What insight have you acquired from this chapter?

Additional Reading

MacCulloch, Diarmaid. *The Reformation*. New York: Viking Penguin, 2003.

Marty, Martin. *Martin Luther*. New York: Viking Penguin, 2004.

McGrath, Alister. *Christianity's Dangerous Idea*. New York: Harper One, 2007.

CHAPTER 4

Reason Two: Personal Relationship with Jesus

1. What conceptions of Evangelicalism did you have before moving toward your current church?
2. What kind of life-changing moment, perhaps as an adolescent or adult, resulted in your "conversion" to faith in Christ?
3. If you feel comfortable describing your experience, take a few minutes to share your conversion story with others in your group.
4. What Catholic rules or customs have you found particularly troubling or confusing?
5. What passages of Scripture have helped you to understand the message of the gospel? How did they help?
6. What insight have you acquired from this chapter?

Additional Reading

St. Augustine. *Confessions*.

Bunyan, John. *Pilgrim's Progress*.

Edwards, Jonathan. *The Religious Affections*. Edinburgh: Banner of Truth Trust, 1991.

CHAPTER 5

Reason Three: Direct Access to God

1. Of what significance is it that Jesus refers to his disciples as his friends in John 15?
2. What portion of Scripture has illuminated your appreciation of the direct nature of God's presence for those who are in Christ?
3. How can the church preserve a sense of personal devotion to God without allowing it to degenerate into sloppy irreverence?
4. How have the Catholic clergy (priests and nuns) positively impacted your life?
5. Why does the idea of succession lead Catholics to the conclusion of "papal infallibility," the notion that the pope can define dogma in a fully authoritative and inerrant manner?
6. Why is direct access to God a critical reality for Christian worship and service?
7. What insight have you acquired from this chapter?

Additional Reading

Kostenberger, Andreas J., and Peter T. O'Brien. *Salvation to the Ends of the Earth.* Downers Grove, IL: InterVarsity, 2001.

Lewis, C. S. *Mere Christianity.*

CHAPTER 6

A Portrait of Catholic Faith: Loyola and Contarini

1. Around what question did Contarini's spiritual struggle revolve? Can you relate?
2. What lessons are offered by the Colloquy of Regensburg?
3. Why is Luther called ex-Catholic, Ignatius called traditional Catholic, and Contarini called Evangelical Catholic?
4. Where do you see examples of these profiles among Catholics today?

5. How do your struggles communicating with Catholic loved ones and friends resemble the obstacles to unity encountered at Regensburg?
6. What insight have you acquired from this chapter?

Additional Reading

Dickens, A. G. *The Counter Reformation*. New York: Norton, 1968.

Gleason, Elizabeth. *Gasparo Contarini: Venice, Rome, and Reform*. Los Angeles: Univ. of California Press, 1993.

CHAPTER 7

Reason Four: Christ-Centered Devotion

1. What is *nuda Scriptura*?
2. If possible, cite an example of where you have observed *nuda Scriptura*.
3. How does the Catholic understanding of the "body of Christ" differ from a typical Evangelical conception?
4. How does Catholic tradition usurp the teaching of Scripture?
5. Cite some examples of how Evangelical teaching may trump Scripture.
6. What consequences result from your answers to questions four and five?
7. What insight have you acquired from this chapter?

Additional Reading

Mahaney, C. J. *The Cross Centered Life*. Sisters, OR: Multnomah, 2002.

Morris, Leon. *The Apostolic Preaching of the Cross*. 1965; Grand Rapids, MI: Eerdmans, 1998.

CHAPTER 8

Reason Five: Motivated by Grace Instead of Guilt

1. What aspects of Andy Brucato's testimony struck you as familiar?
2. What is the "great exchange" as Andy describes it?
3. To what extent have you struggled with an injurious form of Catholic guilt?
4. If you are comfortable doing so, explain how you have dealt with the problem.
5. What is Luther's "Dung Hill" and how does it illustrate the doctrine of justification?
6. How could an Evangelical pastor (who is doctrinally sound) ever preach a message titled "Why I Believe in Purgatory"?
7. What insight have you acquired from this chapter?

Additional Reading

Hill, Charles E., and Frank A. James III, eds. *The Glory of the Atonement*. Downers Grove, IL: InterVarsity, 2004.

Stott, John. *The Cross of Christ*. Downers Grove, IL: InterVarsity, 1986.

CHAPTER 9

How Catholics View Evangelicals

1. Why would a Catholic accuse Evangelicalism of reducing salvation to "fire insurance"?
2. What did the Protestant Reformers teach about good works?
3. How does their emphasis on obedience relate to their insistence on justification by "faith alone"?
4. Identify some valuable lessons that Evangelicals can learn from Catholics.
5. What are major criticisms that Catholics have of Evangelicals?
6. Of the critiques mentioned in the previous question, which one is regarded as most noticeable by your Catholic friends and loved ones?

7. What can you do to improve the way your Catholic friends and family view your Evangelical faith?
8. What insight have you acquired from this chapter?

Additional Reading

Howard, Thomas. *Evangelical Is Not Enough: Worship of God in Liturgy and Sacrament.* San Francisco: Ignatius, 1984.

CHAPTER 10

Traditional, Evangelical, and Cultural Catholics

1. Why must Evangelicals communicate the gospel to Catholics?
2. What are some characteristics of traditional Catholics?
3. What are some areas of sensitivity to be aware of when addressing traditional Catholics?
4. What are the two prominent values that Evangelical Protestants share with Evangelical Catholics?
5. What are the distinctive qualities of cultural Catholics?
6. How would you approach a discussion about Jesus if you were sitting down with an Evangelical Catholic?
7. How might your approach differ if you were speaking with a cultural Catholic?
8. What insight have you acquired from this chapter?

Additional Reading

Green, Michael. *Sharing Your Faith with Your Friends and Family.* Grand Rapids, MI: Baker, 2005.

CHAPTER 11

How to Relate to Catholics with Grace and Truth

1. Of the seven different ways that Evangelicals view Catholics, which one best describes your understanding?
2. What aspects of the definition of *evangelism* did you find most helpful?

3. Which of the "red light" mistakes have you committed?
4. Which elements of the "yellow light" section have you found applicable?
5. Describe a fruitful conversation you have had with a Catholic friend or loved one. What made it fruitful?
6. What is the "main thing" in our discussions with Catholics?
7. What insight have you acquired from this chapter?

Additional Reading

Lindsay, Art. *Love, the Ultimate Apologetic: The Heart of Christian Witness*. Downers Grove, IL: InterVarsity, 2008.

Stackhouse, John G., Jr., *Humble Apologetics: Defending the Faith Today*. Oxford: Oxford Univ. Press, 2002.

CHAPTER 12

Glorify God and Enjoy Him Forever

1. What comes to mind when you think about God? How does this concept of God relate to the person and passion of Jesus?
2. Why is the Old Testament so vital to the church?
3. What does God's covenant faithfulness to Israel teach us about his character?
4. Why does God correct Peter in Matthew 17:5? How does this exhortation speak to the church today?
5. Explain the practical significance of the upsilon vector.
6. What is the good news of Matthew 17:6–8?
7. What insight have you acquired from this chapter?

Additional Reading

Lewis, C. S. *Surprised by Joy*.

Moody, Josh. *The God Centered Life: Insights from Jonathan Edwards for Today*. Vancouver: Regent, 2006.

Piper, John. *Desiring God: Meditations of a Christian Hedonist*. Sisters, OR: Multnomah, 1996.

INDEX

WRITTEN BY DYLAN PAHMAN

Note: page numbers in italics refer to illustrations; page numbers with an *n* refer to footnotes; page numbers with an *s* refer to excursus sidebars; page numbers with a *t* refer to tables.

Share Your Thoughts

With the Author: Your comments will be forwarded to the author when you send them to *zauthor@zondervan.com.*

With Zondervan: Submit your review of this book by writing to *zreview@zondervan.com.*

Free Online Resources at

www.zondervan.com

Zondervan AuthorTracker: Be notified whenever your favorite authors publish new books, go on tour, or post an update about what's happening in their lives.

Daily Bible Verses and Devotions: Enrich your life with daily Bible verses or devotions that help you start every morning focused on God.

Free Email Publications: Sign up for newsletters on fiction, Christian living, church ministry, parenting, and more.

Zondervan Bible Search: Find and compare Bible passages in a variety of translations at www.zondervanbiblesearch.com.

Other Benefits: Register yourself to receive online benefits like coupons and special offers, or to participate in research.